WHAT READERS ARE SAYING...

"Valerie's story takes us on what could be a heart wrenching journey, but turns into a powerful step-by-step approach toward building a future for children and families dealing with autism spectrum disorder. She touches into the personal, familial, societal, and religious minefields in order to guide us to safer ground with one another. Rather than putting her arms around the reader, she gives the reader a road map for navigating this modern day terrain. Hooray for the solid ground Valerie provides! She has done her work well in order to provide a brighter future for children with special needs."

Luanne Somers, BA, MA,
Classical Homeopath Somers Healing & Consulting
somersconnect.com

"As a mother of a child with significant special needs, I completely understand the sense of isolation and overwhelm Valerie experienced. I applaud her commitment to sharing her experience and expertise to pave the road for all the parents who follow behind us. I could have saved years of legal battles if I had the advice she presents in this book!"

Niki Elliott, Ph.D.
Founder and CEO of Innerlight Sanctuary, LLC
Author of *The Intuitive Mother*

"This is a must-read for any parent with a special needs child. Valerie's journey takes us gently through the maze of advocating for our angels while teaching us to see our children as the teachers they truly are. Thank you, Valerie."

Angela Gonzales, MD
Founder of Renaissance Mind
and Dr. Angie's Place

"As an educator and mother of a special needs angel, I found this to be a miraculous book, summarizing but not missing pertinent aspects of advocating for a fully inclusive life for a special needs loved one. Valerie validated the frustrations of educators who are forced to adhere to outdated policies while attempting to teach to each child's unique style of learning in various settings, and empowered parents to take the practical and emotional journey through the experience of parenting such an angel. In just a few hundred pages of her beautiful story, she was able to weave the varied components of guiding families through the education system, community, and religious organizations and the spiritual principles that enabled her to advocate for her daughter and for my son, who is now graduating from high school with a diploma. This book is a gift in compassion and understanding that differently-abled people are embodied Love, and that we can all find our wings and create a better world."

Karen Aceves
Parent, Client, Educator

"What a beautiful true story of an amazing mother and daughter, and the will to fight for and believe in your child! Valerie and Chanel's journey through Autism and conquering it is inspiring and hopeful to all of us in similar situations. Thank you, Valerie, for sharing your valuable story and advice! I was greatly moved and inspired!"

Dr. Gowri Rocco

"As a working mother of an autistic son, I always worry. As an educator, I thought I knew what to do. Yet I was constantly feeling frustrated with my inability to get my son the services he needed. I realized that my educational experience wasn't enough, and I needed help. Valerie was kind, compassionate, and someone who TRULY understood what I was going through. She guided me and taught me how to advocate for my son and his educational rights. He is now on the road to a successful high school education, and I owe so much of that to her. While reading this book, I found myself feeling emotional. I wasn't alone in the struggles I was going through. *Advocating for Your Special Needs Angel* reminded me that I can be vulnerable yet strong, and that we all struggle, but must not give up. I would recommend this book for all the parents out there struggling to learn how to advocate for their child and searching to know that they are not alone."

Shannan Ash
Classroom Teacher, Client,
Mother of Autistic Angel

"Advocating for Your Special Needs Angel is a well-written guide to special education services describing the struggle commonly encountered by parents of and students with special needs. This exceptional guide is a must-read for all families involved in navigating a challenging set of supports and services."

Russell G. Rankin
Past Executive Director, Area Boards 12,
California State Council on Developmental Disabilities

"Advocating for Your Special Needs Angel is a must-read for parents, teachers, therapists, and doctors. Valerie not only demonstrates what is possible when we see the strengths in our children, but she provides a step-by-step guide for parents in working with Special Education Services. This is truly an inspirational story for all."

JoQueta Handy
Handy Wellness and COB Learning Center,
Author of *Brilliant Learning* and
BrilliantLearningOnline.com

"In her new book, *Advocating for Your Special Needs Angel: A Mother and Special Education Advocate's Practical Guide to Helping Children Find Their Wings,* Valerie reveals her deepest emotions as a mother and the way in which she found the strength and determination to fiercely advocate for her children with special needs. Her story provides hope and insights for other families on their journey and an understanding of the motivation and information that fuels Valerie's unwavering support as an advocate for them."

Susanne Smith Roley
OTD, OTR/L, FAOTA, private occupational therapist, co-founder of the nonprofit educational organization, Collaborative for Leadership in Ayres Sensory Integration (CLASI), and co-author of *Sensory Integration: Applying Clinical Reasoning to Practice...*

"Whew! Valerie's book helped me to see all of my unprocessed grief, anger, and desperation. But more importantly, Valerie gifted me and every reader with knowledge, power, activation, and HOPE, which I absolutely needed! *Advocating For Your Special Needs Angel* is a must-read for every parent walking this daunting path with your child. Regardless of where you are in the journey, this book meets you there and encourages you to keep fighting the good fight!"

Marlia Cochran
Author, Speaker, Pastor
& Mama to a Special Needs Angel

"You never really know what people are going through, nor how powerful women are. This book is heroism, perseverance, grace, and unconditional love!"

Leeza Villagomez
President of Yoga Den, Inc.
Author of *Yoga Drunk*

Advocating for Your Special Needs Angel

A Mother and Special Education
Advocate's Practical Guide to Helping
Children Find Their Wings

by

Valerie Aprahamian

Advocates for Angels

Advocating for Your Special Needs Angel

A Mother and Special Education Advocate's
Practical Guide to Helping Children Find Their Wings

Published by
Advocates for Angels
Corona, California

www.AdvocatesForAngels.com

Copyright © 2016 *by Valerie Aprahamian*

Cover Design by Dan Mulhern Design
Interior Design by Dawn Teagarden

ISBN-13:978-1530497973

ISBN-10:1530497973

Printed in the United States of America

www.AdvocatesForAngels.com

*To my beautiful daughter, my angel, Jessica.
On the day you were born, everyone said you
had the face of an angel. At the age of
twenty-eight, you earned your wings.*

*To my second angel, Chanel.
Being your mother has transformed my life
beyond my wildest dreams. Thank you for being
my hero and my most powerful teacher.*

ACKNOWLEDGMENTS

To my angel, Chanel Lee, you were the inspiration for this book. Thank you for being who you are in the world. Everyone you come into contact with is changed by your presence through your authenticity, honesty, and purity. Every day of your life, as you engaged in the never-ending hours of your program to receive special education, therapies, and tutoring, your unwavering diligence to do your very best without complaint makes you my hero. And you know why you are here: To raise the consciousness of the planet with (as you call them) "your special powers."

To my daughter, Jessica Faye, you were the catalyst for this book. Your life and death has transformed every level of my being, as I was stripped of everything that was not love. You have been my most powerful teacher, who has constantly challenged me to "go deeper." Because of your message to "Follow My Heart," I found the courage to expand my perception of the spiritual path, heal myself, fulfill my passion and purpose, and experience myself as unrecognizable to the person I once was. You are truly and quite literally my angel in heaven.

To my daughter, Celeste Ann, you never fail to astonish me with the depth of your capacity to love deeply and your sensitive, intuitive nature that always shows up when I need it most. Even though you were younger than Chanel, you took on the "big sister" role with grace and ease when you were only three years old. Thank you for teaching me acceptance. Your ability to express your undeniable love for life through song is a true gift to the world. You are a shining star.

To my son, Michael John, you are the epitome of inclusion and non-judgment, and you were born that way. You are never too busy to do something to help Chanel, whether it is making her a meal, engaging her in conversation, or driving her to a destination. Compassion and tolerance are just a part of your being. You approach life full of wonder and intelligence that fills me with overwhelming gratitude.

To Symphony Angelic, thank you for your dry humor and the loads of fun you have brought into my life, and for teaching me to let go of expectations and increase my capacity to trust more fully. On the day you were born, your mommy said it was the happiest day of her life…and it truly was.

To my husband, Michael, thank you for stepping up with the kids and filling in for me when I was moving through the grief process and tirelessly dedicated to the system reform. Your love and support were the only way I could have done both while the kids remained healthy and happy.

To Alisha, thank you for the loving kindness and open heart that you have offered to Chanel, year after year, since grade school. You have been Chanel's only friend who has included her and accepted her always, with open arms.

Even though you are now paid to be Chanel's job coach and aide, you approach your job with love and friendship that money could not purchase with any paycheck. You have been a true blessing to Chanel and our entire family.

To Jamie, you were the company owner that I had envisioned so many years ago when I came to the realization that State Disability agencies would not be able to place Chanel in competitive employment that would fulfill her soul. Thank you for being that employer who refuses to discriminate against those who are different. You are one of the very few who hold the perception to see and support Chanel's many strengths, talents, and abilities without limitations. Because of you, Chanel has been trained and will be hired for the job of her dreams and receive the same wages her peers do.

To Leeza, my beloved Yoga teacher and friend. You were the door that opened me up to making space for changing the way I perceive my religious beliefs. Through my yoga practice, I learned how to peel the layers of judgment, polarity, and separation. Thank you for being my travel buddy on the transformative journey to India, where I was finally able to find the healing I needed for the passing of my daughter. Yoga has changed my life forever, and I will be eternally grateful for the physical, mental, emotional, and energetic teaching you have offered me.

To Linda, you are the district administrator that changed everything, not only for my family but for all families in our community. Thank you for having the integrity, devotion, and perseverance to gracefully change the way the district works with parents to meet the needs of all students. The respect and gratitude I hold for you cannot be put into words, but is revealed in the students' lives you have transformed because you had the power to make the decisions to give them a successful education.

To Dr. Gowri Rocco, without you, I would not have been healthy and strong as I moved through those difficult transitional years. You were a key player in helping me to learn how to take care of myself on my journey to find balance and well-being. Thank you for your listening ear as I cried in your office and for being my number one cheerleader as you championed my every success. You are an extraordinary doctor that embodies the definition of holistic medical practice.

To Amanda and your team, because of you and your undeniable gifts and talents, this book is now a reality. Thank you for your patience, encouragement, and support from manuscript to publishing. Thank you, Amanda, for holding my vision for the book and for having the ability to keep me grounded when I had doubt and felt overwhelmed. You made it possible for me to combine all the "layers" of my story into a graceful sequential flow to communicate the power and purpose of my mission and the evolutionary gift of our angels.

To all the kids and their parents whom I have had the profound honor to work with over the years, you have not only made my job incredibly fulfilling but have allowed me to live my purpose in this life. Your kids have been my greatest teachers. Many of you have become lifelong friends as we have walked the journey as parents together. This book is the result of all our stories but, most importantly, it is the collective message of all the special needs population.

CONTENTS

Introduction: Angel Awakening......................19

Chapter 1: Fall from Grace...........................33

Chapter 2: Chariots of Fury 63

Chapter 3: Trumpets of Justice 101

Chapter 4: Tear Drops from Heaven 129

Chapter 5: Angel Gifts................................173

Epilogue: Angel in Flight............................201

About Valerie..209

A Special Invitation from Valerie 213

"If I only had the eyes to see as you see,
the courage to love purely,
and the patience not to judge others,
then I would have learned
what you have come here to teach me.

Your entire life, each and everyday,
you gave your all and you never gave up.
With unwavering determination,
you have shared your wisdom and truth,
not by the words you speak, but by the heavenly
message that permeates your being
to create for us a ncw Earth."

Valerie Aprahamian

INTRODUCTION

ANGEL AWAKENING

Chanel and Valerie

Chanel

"There she is! Look, over there!" We all screamed, "Chanel!" as we waved our arms to get her attention. Searching the crowd of thousands of faces for her family, her eyes finally met ours and she waved back with a huge smile on her delighted face. Her brown eyes radiated pride and her slim, beautiful body literally bounced with joy as she walked across the field in her graduation gown with her high school class.

I felt as if I was in another dimension, almost in disbelief. *Wow, this is really happening...Chanel is actually graduating from high school...with a diploma...with honors.*

It was the goal I had set for Chanel fifteen years prior, when everyone else told me she wouldn't be able to progress or experience success. I was witnessing my vision achieved as I watched Chanel beaming with happiness. It was as though she was floating on air as she glided up to the stage to receive her diploma. It was truly surreal. For my beautiful angel Chanel, and for me, it was a glorious moment of triumph.

It was validation that what I believed in my heart, in every fiber of my being, was really true, and it was confirmation that I was right in making my own decisions to follow my heart, no matter what others said.

I did not allow the limiting recommendations of assessment findings to detour me on my mission. I did not believe the bleak diagnosis of doctors and educators, year after year, throughout Chanel's education. I didn't allow them to label Chanel with "disability" as her identity. And I didn't give in to the fear, anger, or depression that I experienced along the way.

No, it wasn't easy, baby girl, but look at how far we've come...

As I watched her sit down with such satisfaction emanating from her face, I couldn't help but think back to those first few years of our special needs journey—the crisis of the diagnosis, the anger of dealing with such broken medical and educational systems, the hard work of negotiating our reality on every human level, the sadness of feeling misunderstood and alone, and eventually that beautiful time when we all finally got on the same page and started to see Chanel progress and thrive in spite of what the professionals told me year after year.

Baby girl, you worked so hard...with such unwavering determination...day after day filled with tutors, therapists, and behavior intervention. From early morning until bedtime, you never gave up and you met every challenge that was placed before you. No matter how hard the task, you always did your best and gave everything you had in order to succeed. You were an inspiration to me as I walked my own journey as your mommy.

The Truth about The Journey

Like all parents of a special needs child, I was faced with what appeared to be insurmountable challenges as I had to quite literally and practically walk a profound journey of grief...twice.

First, I walked the journey with my firstborn daughter, Jessica, who was born with ADHD, bipolar and seizure disorder. I had no idea what I was doing, but I learned quickly. I had to. My daughter's well-being was at stake. I searched for the right therapies and supports, and she was making really beautiful progress, up until her sudden death at the young age of twenty-eight.

That grief journey was a mother's worse nightmare, but after many years of self-reflection and unwavering determination to heal, I learned how to move through it. Today, I continue to take another type of grief journey with my daughter Chanel, who at the time of this book publication is twenty-four.

The difference between the grief of a special needs parent and the grief experienced as a result of losing a child is this: while the intense grief of losing a child eventually changes with time, the cycle of grief continues throughout the special needs child's life as they move through each milestone in the lifecycle and we watch them miss out on 'normal.' (Now I don't really like to use the label "normal" because it creates a comparison that judges our kids to be viewed as "less than," and this is absolutely not my intention. I use this word to relay to you the expectations that we all hold as parents regarding the future of our child.)

Over the years, I've found that no one tells any of us that this grief is part of what we're facing as parents of special needs children, so we get caught up in the details of "What do I do now?" And as we move into action, and try to keep up with all of the special needs requirements and routines, it is easy to avoid dealing with our feelings and moving through this grief process with awareness while still advocating for our angels and helping them find their wings.

Chanel is a young adult now, and the cycle of grief continues for me. During each big moment in Chanel's life, the cycle will begin again. For example, my niece recently got married, and our entire family attended the wedding. Beneath my joy and celebration lay the realization that Chanel, most likely, may never marry and have a family of her own. And so the grief bubbles up once again.

The same question will always arise, "What will Chanel's future hold? What will happen to her when my husband and I are no longer here?" As the children of family, friends, neighbors, and business associates move through the typical lifecycle, Chanel is left behind because she has a developmental disability called autism.

Even though I have these moments of grief that sometimes reappear as life continues, I have learned how to move through the grief with awareness and understanding.

Because of my years of advocacy and experience as a mother of a young lady with the diagnosis of autism, I have found some keys to moving through all of the stages of grief more quickly and easily. (Half the battle is knowing that this is what you're really doing.)

With this awareness and these keys, you can give yourself the love, understanding, and acceptance you need to take care of yourself as you move through the grief cycle and advocate for your child's wings.

Nothing and No One
Prepares You for This...Until Now

Like every parent of a newly diagnosed child, I found myself in a whole new universe of special education, service providers, doctors, and government agencies. And I quickly learned, as most parents do, that I lacked the knowledge and understanding I needed to successfully navigate the system.

But I was determined to change that...

Over the past eighteen years, I have not only walked the journey as my own daughter's advocate, I have become the "go-to person" in my community to teach other parents how to advocate for their angels as well. As I learned how to support Chanel in finding her wings, I continued to educate myself to become a successful non-attorney advocate. I learned everything I could, as quickly as I could. I attended conferences and classes and spent countless hours every day reading books and researching special education law. At the same time, I was gaining my experience in assisting families through the IEP (Individualized Education Program) process. Essentially, I educated myself and acquired thousands of hours of on-the-job advocacy experience that would be comparable to that of a masters program.

Simply put, after representing hundreds of families and attending close to two thousand IEP meetings, I've learned (sometimes the hard way) powerful skills, tools, and strategies to support these special children through their journey.

I soon realized that in order to meet the need of the mass amount of parents and children who need this type of support, I had to write a book and get everything on paper—to give the parents the education, inspiration, strategies, and tools they need to support their angels. I wanted to tell the story that we all share as parents of special needs children. And as you read this book, you will see that we all go through much of the very same experience. It's not just my story—it's OUR story!

But most importantly, I want to help parents walk this journey with awareness and create unity within their own families.

You may be asking, "How can I accomplish this?" The answer is simple: "By using every experience on your journey as an opportunity to 'know yourself.'" Through each step, you have a choice to react to your situation with feelings of fear, anger, and self-doubt; or instead, make the choice to know yourself as capable, happy, and filled with well-being.

In order to educate, inspire, and equip you as you read, I have included:

- **Information**: This is the educational information that I find many parents of special needs children don't have. I've integrated a lot of it into my story, so you'll learn it as you read how I learned it, and I've put some of the additional advocacy information in the gray-scale boxes throughout the book.

- **My Story**: I've shared all of the most important moments from my journey as a parent of an autistic angel—the good, the bad, and the downright ugly—to show you that if I can do it, you can do it too... emotionally, mentally, physically, and even spiritually. As a mother and a non-attorney advocate, I also continued to experience all of the everyday life experiences that continued to unfold around me and within me. I know the challenges many of you are facing because I lived through them too—a challenged marriage, financial crises, health problems, isolation, crumbling relationships, and even self-doubt in my relationship with and perception of God...and therefore, myself.

• **Tools and Strategies**: I've included many of the tools and strategies that I share with every parent who reaches out for my support. Any time that you see a question or an exercise, please answer/do it. These don't work if they're not used.

Autistic and Special Needs Angels

Throughout the book, even though I may use the specific term "autistic spectrum," I am also speaking of all children who may not necessarily have the specific diagnosis of *autism*. This includes the kids with the diagnosis of ADHD, Emotional Disturbance, Learning Disabilities, Cerebral Palsy, and all other neurological disorders. I simply use the label *autism spectrum disorder*, because that is the diagnosis that is most prevalent in our world today. It is my belief that many of these kids, no matter the diagnosis, are energetically sensitive.

A New Paradigm

Autism has now reached 1 in every 68 children born today (1 in 42 boys) and the numbers continue to grow rapidly. Doctors continue to say that the cause is inconclusive, even though there is much evidence right in front of our noses. While the medical realm continues to argue about autism's origin, I believe we are missing the bigger picture of this worldwide epidemic.

What if their presence and immense rise in numbers are a wakeup call for our world today? What if, just as every child is a mirror for their parent, the autistic child is also that mirror, with the ultimate purpose of raising humanity's awareness to live with compassion and unconditional love?

As families, educational systems, health care providers, and society in general continue to struggle with making the changes necessary to accommodate this population, we must ask ourselves, "What is the lesson we can learn from this remarkable evolutionary process that continues to grow exponentially year after year?"

After working with hundreds of families of children and adults with autism as well as raising my own daughter, Chanel, I have come to understand that my most profound lesson has been this: *These special angels are not here for us to "fix" them. They are not broken or disordered or disabled.* This is not to say that specialized therapy, educational programs, special diets, or behavioral intervention is not necessary or effective. We know that these interventions can assist them greatly by helping them to be more present in their own bodies and, therefore, help them to function more comfortably in our world. In fact, the primary purpose of my advocacy career is to assist parents in developing the most appropriate educational program, which includes many forms of therapy and medical interventions. Yet, it remains my personal opinion that if we can change the way we look at these individuals, they can then become our very powerful teachers.

It's Possible for All of Us

I believe that learning and integrating the content of this book will change, or maybe even confirm, your perspective about your special angel and make the possibilities for your child easier for them to achieve.

And it's important that I let you know what to expect while you're reading.

As you read this book, it may cause you to awaken to a realm of emotions such as fear, anxiety, anger, frustration, and maybe even hopelessness, but don't let these emotions scare you. They're normal, and it's good for you to feel them and learn from them. You may want to throw this book and scream, or be tempted to give up, but my promise is that if you persevere and give yourself the patience you need to get through to the end of my story, and you do the work as you go, you will not be disappointed. The feelings will be intense at first, but they will diminish and eventually leave you. In their place, you will develop feelings such as confidence, gratitude, well-being, abundance, and cooperation. You have what you need inside of you to dig deep and do this work, and you will receive the tools, information and inspiration you are looking for to advocate for your special angel…and, in the process, I believe you can transform your life…and find your own wings.

Watching Chanel cross that platform and receive her diploma was the culmination of my journey of transformation and my promise to stay true to myself by "following my heart." I created a different life for my child against all odds. "Why?" the ever-present question that pulsed within my being had been answered and taken form as the gift of my extraordinary daughter, Chanel Lee.

And the same amazing transformative experience can happen for you…

"Trials are not arbitrary.

When I speak about them,
I am referring to the mindful suffering.

Man has come to his present development
thanks to his hardships and trials.

These are what prepare man for
the Coming of Love."

Peter Deunov

CHAPTER 1

FALL
FROM GRACE

Valerie, just stay calm, I coached myself to try and stay balanced as I noticed my head was swimming with the last minute details that still needed attention for the bible study dinner we were hosting. My nerves were getting the best of me, and my stomach was tied in a knot as I moved at superhuman speed.

I was deep in multitasking mode as I juggled five different jobs at once in a race against time before our guests arrived. Like many moms, this was just a way of life for me and it came rather naturally. I kept my eye on the lasagna to make sure it didn't overcook, set each table, wiped down the kitchen counters, picked up the living room, and reminded my husband to make sure he changed into a clean shirt. My eldest daughter, Jessica, was helping her grandma take care of Chanel, who had been sick for a few days.

As I picked up a baby toy I saw hiding in the corner of the room, my mind drifted to my baby girl. *She's been sick with a fever for days now. I hate those vaccinations. It's awful to watch your 22-month-old baby scream with every needle pinch… And these fevers… They shouldn't last this long, right?*

I was looking around the room, feeling like I was finally ready for my guests, when I heard my mother-in-law scream, "Something's wrong with Chanel! Michael, Valerie! Something's wrong with Chanel!"

Her panicked voice filled me with terror as I raced toward the stairs. With every step, the knot in my stomach tightened. Nothing could have prepared me for what I saw.

My sweet baby girl's tiny body was jerking and twisting when my terrified mother-in-law placed Chanel in my arms. She was wrapped in her blanket and burning up with fever.

What's wrong with her? What do I do?

We called 911 and waited for what seemed like an eternity. All I could do was hold Chanel in my arms and pray as I paced back and forth and cried out toward the heavens, "Please, God, help Chanel. Hold her in your arms. Heal her…protect her. Please, God, stop this seizure."

Our guests watched and prayed as I stepped into the back of the ambulance, holding Chanel in my arms. The screaming siren only added to my terror as I watched the paramedics strip Chanel of her blanket and clothes to examine her while she continued to seize.

Shoving my fear aside, I tried to comfort my baby, "I'm here, Honey. Mommy is right here with you. You're going to be alright, Chanel. Mommy is here."

We were escorted into a cubical in the emergency room where we waited again. For hours, no one seemed to be alarmed or act as if my child was in danger.

Why aren't the doctors doing something? Chanel is lying lifeless in my arms and it's been over two hours since the seizure. Why aren't they calling for a specialist or ordering some kind of testing?

Chanel's seizure had lasted for more than twenty minutes. I knew in my gut that something was terribly wrong, but the paramedics assured me that she had experienced a febrile seizure and nothing more. But it didn't make sense.

That can't be true. Febrile seizures aren't this violent and don't last this long. A few of my friends' children had experienced febrile seizures, and the way they described it was nothing like what I had witnessed with Chanel.

Fear gripped my being as we waited in the emergency room for more than three hours.

In the end, the doctor sent us home, stating that she had experienced a typical "febrile seizure" as a result of pneumonia and that there was nothing to worry about. As a mother, I knew they were wrong. I knew that this was not a simple febrile seizure and that something terrible had just occurred in Chanel's body that would change the course of our lives forever.

What Happened to My Baby?

It didn't take long to realize that the appropriate speech that Chanel had developed in the first 18 months of her life had virtually disappeared. After Chanel woke up from her seizure, she never spoke another word of her own. The little speech she did display was "echolalia," which is a form of verbalizations that are memorized by the child, usually derived from videos or phrases they've heard somewhere. The child repeats the memorized quote over and over in the same voice and manner in which they initially heard it.

I always found it so interesting how Chanel could recall a quote or line from a video and use it to communicate in a situation or conversation so perfectly. The quote she would repeat would actually communicate her wants, needs, and thoughts as it pertained to what was happening around her. It was fascinating how she had the capacity to memorize so many quotes in her little brain and could retrieve them at the precise moment in a conversation in order to communicate, but it wasn't typical, and I knew it.

Why isn't she using words like other children?

In addition to her speech regression, Chanel developed other behaviors over the next eighteen months. She lost eye contact and seemed to retreat into her own isolated world. When she found herself in a loud environment, she covered her ears and screamed. In fact, she would disappear into another room when there were too many people and too much conversation and noise. Often times, I would find her sitting in front of the TV and staring off into space, lost in her own little world. Despite my best efforts to play with her and read books to her—to connect with her again—she wasn't interested. She preferred to play alone and showed little interest in interacting with me or anyone else.

Where did my little bundle of laughter and play go?

At night, when I would tuck her in, I would look into her eyes and try to connect with the baby girl I once knew. I would beg her to look at me and say something, anything, but she would look away as if it was too painful to look into her own mommy's eyes.

I didn't know it then, but all of these behaviors and symptoms are typical for a child with the diagnosis of autism.

As I closed the door to her room, I cried tears of grief and fear.

What will tomorrow bring for my sweet little angel? I have to find out what really happened to Chanel and how I can help her.

Chanel is...What?!?

I sat in the waiting room, feeling consumed with dread, while Chanel was being assessed.

I know that seizure did something to Chanel. When she opened her eyes after she slept for three hours, she was never the same. She doesn't look at or talk to me anymore. She's in her own little world. Why can't the doctors see that Chanel's development has suffered as a result of that seizure that happened after she got her vaccination shots more than a year ago?

An entire team of developmental pediatricians sat behind a glass window and observed Chanel as she played in a room full of toys, assisted by a play therapist. Chanel wasn't talking or interacting with others in a typical three-year-old way.

"Chanel has a developmental disability called 'autism,'" the doctor began. "She will most likely never learn to read or write, nor will she ever be verbal." She placed her hand on my leg, as if to brace me, "You might even begin thinking about institutionalizing her at some point."

My body went completely numb with shock and confusion as I looked around the room at the colorful building blocks, the dolls and cars, and other toys organized carefully and so perfectly categorized in boxes around this medical playroom.

What on earth is she talking about? I don't care if she's a UCLA doctor! Chanel was a beautiful, curly-haired, brown-eyed, Shirley Temple look-alike. She was the perfect baby—

sweet and quiet and compliant. Never gave me any problem with crying, sleeping, or eating. She smiled and laughed and was a happy baby. How could this stranger, a doctor who is an "expert" in child development, give me this diagnosis about my beautiful baby girl?!?

I tried to comprehend the doctor's devastating words as she continued to talk about autism and how it would affect Chanel's future. Her words began to run together and fade in and out, as if I was watching a scene in an old movie in slow motion. A wave of nausea rolled over me and made it impossible to focus on her robotic, matter of fact, monotone voice. But, throughout my entire body, I felt the message she was delivering and it felt like a death sentence.

"But doctor, don't you think that the seizure she had caused this? She was fine until that first seizure. She talked and acted like a typical child until that seizure after she had her vaccinations. All of this has to be linked to that seizure!" I relayed my concern that they weren't considering the history and sequence of events that had occurred.

I knew that the first seizure was the onset of her problem, but no one would believe me. Her pediatrician, the neurologist, the team at UCLA—none of them would connect her initial seizure to the fact that Chanel was now being diagnosed with autism. All their responses sounded rehearsed, "There is no correlation between the seizure and the onset of autism. It is typical for children to be diagnosed between the ages of 22 and 28 months. Many children diagnosed with autism also have a seizure disorder."

What is wrong with these people?

As I waited in the examination room at the pediatrician's office, I felt my anxiety rising at the thought of giving my baby more of those horrible vaccines and simply couldn't contain it. "Doctor, after Chanel received her last shots, she developed pneumonia with a 105 degree temperature. She had a seizure that lasted almost 20 minutes and we ended up in the emergency room. Since then, she hasn't spoken a word and now she has been diagnosed with autism! I am really concerned and scared to give her another round of vaccinations."

"Mrs. Aprahamian," the doctor responded with an arrogant, even scornful, tone. "There is absolutely no reason to believe that her last immunizations had anything to do with an onset of autism. Children need their vaccinations… the nurse will be right in."

Against my better judgment, while trying to fight the nagging sense of danger that filled the pit of my stomach, I complied with the doctor's orders.

I didn't know it then, but the Pediatric community had not yet acquired the knowledge needed to understand or treat children with the diagnosis. Today, parents have access to the knowledge and information available to make an informed decision before consenting to vaccinating their child. Unfortunately, I was faced with making this decision more than twenty years ago and, therefore, I wasn't given that choice.

It was 1994 and autism was just beginning to show up in kids across the country. It was called "high functioning autism," which meant that the child had developed "autistic like" behaviors around the age of 18 to 28 months.

Intellectually, I could see how Chanel fit into this category perfectly, but I couldn't accept the prognosis. In fact, I was having trouble accepting the diagnosis.

Vaccinations and Autism

According to the Centers for Disease Control and Prevention, 1 in 68 children in the United States has an autism spectrum disorder (ASD). Ten years ago, autism's estimated prevalence was 1 in 166. Today it's 1 in 68 – an increase of more than 100% in one decade.

According to the newest report, the CDC estimates 1 in 42 boys has autism, which is 4.5 times more than girls.

Autism Speaks and many other foundations that support autism research believe differently. Autism Speaks website provides this information regarding prevention, "According to a new government survey of parents suggests that 1 in 45 children, ages 3 through 17, have been diagnosed with autism spectrum disorder (ASD). This is notably higher than the official government estimate of 1 in 68 American children with autism, by Centers for Disease Control and Prevention."

Because the new numbers come from a parent survey, they don't replace the CDC's 1-in-68 figure as the official estimate of autism prevalence in the United States.

Autism Speaks goes on to say, "However, the CDC has acknowledged that its estimate has significant limitations. It's based on an analysis of the medical and school records of eight-year-old children at monitoring sites across the country. As such, it can miss children who are not receiving medical or special education services related to autism."

"The 1 in 45 estimate is not surprising and is likely a more accurate representation of autism prevalence in the United States," comments epidemiologist Michael Rosanoff, Autism Speaks director for public health research. "This means that 2 percent of children in the U.S. are living with autism. The earlier they have access to care, services and treatment, the more likely they are to progress."

In its effort to develop better methods for identifying autism and estimating prevalence, Autism Speaks has funded studies using active surveillance methods that go beyond parent reports and record reviews. In the first such study, in South Korea, researchers went into schools to screen children for autism. They found a prevalence of 1 in 38 – with many of the children having gone previously undiagnosed.

"Autism Speaks and the CDC have since collaborated to support a study testing the same active screening methods in a U.S. community. The results are expected in 2016."

"We need to better understand not only who has autism," Rosanoff concludes, "but whether they are receiving the support they need and how we can ensure that they do receive it."

To date, the medical realm continues to state they don't know the cause for the continual alarming rise in children being born with autism. Over the years, some people have had concerns that autism might be linked to an ingredient in vaccines children receive and the increase in vaccine schedule, especially over the past 30 years. One vaccine ingredient that has been studied specifically is thimerosal, which was previously used as a preservative in many recommended childhood vaccines. However, in 2001, thimerosal was supposedly reduced to trace amounts in all childhood vaccines except for one type of influenza vaccine. Evidence from several studies examining trends in vaccine use and changes in autism frequency does not support such an association between thimerosal and autism. (Or so they say.)

All of this information is questionable as the pharmaceutical companies are not mandated to accurately disclose exactly what is in the vaccinations and they are protected from being liable for responsibility of a harmful outcome. Did you know that a lawsuit cannot be filed against a pharmaceutical company?

According to the Canary Party who has joined the National Vaccine Information Center in calling for the repeal of the 1986 National Childhood Vaccine Injury Act, "the 1986 law that prevented Americans from suing Pharmaceutical companies for vaccine injury and death, and established the Vaccine Injury Compensation Program has been a failure. It is time to repeal this legislation."

The Canary Party explains, "This law has allowed vaccine interest to abuse the public trust by pushing less safe and less effective vaccines, ignoring soaring reports of serious adverse vaccine reactions, and bloating the vaccine schedule from 24 doses in the 60's 70's and 80's, to a 69 dose schedule today that is not tested in combination for safety."

"Further, the US Vaccine Injury Compensation Program created to replace the tort system has been a failure, and has done more to protect vaccine profits than it has to care for victims of vaccine injury. The US Government Accounting Office, Stanford Law, American University Law and The Associated Press/NYT have all issued their findings following in depth investigations into the program and agree that the VICP fails to properly compensate vaccine victims."

"Because the public accountability mechanism has ceased to function, vaccine interests, and even doctors in offices, are now making wildly false product safety claims to families, and the public has no way to stop this misinformation campaign by those profiting from the over use and inappropriate use of vaccinations."

"This special liability protection given only to vaccine makers has turned the vaccine business from a 750 million dollar per year industry to a reported 27 billion dollar per year industry, while the health of American children during that same time period has plummeted."

Nevertheless, a review by the Institute of Medicine (IOM) concluded that "the evidence favors rejection of a causal relationship between thimerosal–containing vaccines and autism." CDC supports the IOM conclusion that there is no relationship between vaccines containing thimerosal and autism rates in children.

Despite this data collection from the CDC and IOM, parents continue to believe that there is a link between the onset of autism and vaccines. Many parents believe these "studies" are biased and do not provide solid evidence due to the concern that there were not enough children involved in the study as well as the fact that there have not been enough studies completed.

Like myself, countless parents insist that their child was typically developing until they received their immunizations. The sequence of events in Chanel's young life indicates that there must be a connection between her vaccines and the onset of the autism diagnosis.

Yet this remains an extremely controversial topic in the medical and pharmaceutical community today.

Dr. Brownstein writes about this issue in his newsletter of Holistic Medicine:

"It has been 15 months since a senior CDC scientist, Dr. William Thompson, became a whistleblower when he admitted that a 2004 CDC study was falsified in order to show that there was no link between the MMR vaccine and autism. In August of 2014 Dr. Thompson stated, 'I regret that my coauthors and I omitted statistically significant information in our 2004 article published in the Journal of Pediatrics.'"

"Folks, we have a whistleblower at the CDC who has admitted, under oath that the CDC falsified data in order to deny a link between vaccinations and autism. Furthermore, Dr. Thompson has stated that senior CDC researchers tried to destroy all documents related to this cover-up. Dr. Thompson has saved these documents. It is nearly 15 months later and nothing has happened."

"There have been no Congressional hearings. The mainstream media has refused to talk about it."

"For the Big Pharm-Vaccine Cartel, it is business as usual. Pregnant women, children and others are still told that vaccines are safe even when they contain toxic substances such as mercury, aluminum and formaldehyde. I would like someone to show me a single study that proves it is safe to inject these toxic substances into any living being—especially a pregnant women or a child. The reason I won't see a study is that there are none."

"The 2004 study mentioned above found no link between the MMR vaccine and autism because they omitted crucial data. When the data was included, the study found a 240% increase in autism among African American children and a 69% increase in all children who were vaccinated with the MMR vaccine before 36 months of age."

"Is there any good news here? There is one bit of positive news. One courageous Congressman has spoken in front of Congress twice about this issue. His name is Bill Posey. Dr. Posey is demanding his colleagues call hearings on this matter."

It is important for every parent to do their own research on this subject and come to their own conclusion regarding the connection between vaccines and autism.

Although school districts state that a child cannot register for school without their vaccinations, until just recently, it remained a parent's right to make the decision not to immunize their child based upon religious or ethical standards. As of June 30, 2015, parents could request a waiver in order to allow their child to register and attend school without immunization.

But on June 30, 2015, Governor Brown signed Senate Bill (SB) 277, which mandates beginning on July 1, 2016, SB 277 will no longer permit immunization exemptions based on personal beliefs for children in public and private schools and child care. These requirements are exempt for students in home-based private schools and independent study programs, who do not receive classroom-based instruction and *students on an IEP*.

Senate Bill 277 requires California children who attend private or public schools to be fully vaccinated regardless of their parents' personal or religious beliefs. Non-vaccinated children can attend schools only if they obtain a medical exemption from a doctor.

Private or public child care centers, preschools, elementary schools, and secondary schools cannot admit children unless they are immunized with all vaccinations required at specific grade levels.

The Department of Public Health has indicated that it will issue further guidance on SB 277 to provide clarification of the exemption for students on IEP's. Until the Department of Public Health issues further guidance, it is their recommendation that Districts do not deny any IEP services to qualified students.

The language of SB277 left enforcement and vaccine noncompliance up to the school's governing authority for each district. Orange County's Department of Education's Legal Division interprets that a court order to vaccinate will be an option. Will all California school districts, by way of their legal counsels, be directed to file court orders against noncomplying parents of all school children in 2016? The problem we are facing as parents of special needs children is that it appears to be that California school districts, by way of their legal counsels, have the option to be directed to file court orders against parents of special needs children on IEP's in 2016. These court orders would essentially trump the unvaccinated special needs child's legal right to a Free and Appropriate Public Education (FAPE) in California under the Federal law of the U.S. Department of Education's requirements under Section 504 of The Rehabilitation Act of 1973.

It is a fact that many autistic children are being recovered through detoxification regimens, the rebalancing of the gut flora, and many other synergistic modalities. A common finding is pointing to the child's "autism-like" symptoms manifesting more from toxic overload rather than a genetic deficiency. Children with "autism-like" symptoms being recovered should not be mandated, by anyone's directives, to take on a further toxic burden through vaccinations that potentially contributed to their "autism-like" diagnosis and special needs calcification in the first place. With the signing of Senate Bill 277 by California Governor Jerry Brown, politics will now come before your child's medical freedom in 2016. As the bill is set to take effect, there are many who are actively repealing legislation appearing to have been pushed by heavy pharmaceutical influences. Many parents believe that this bill violates medical ethics in the form of failing to provide a parent's right to informed consent and freedom over their own child's health and well-being.

Conventional medicine has largely failed autistic children and their families. Since those early days when Chanel was first diagnosed, autism went through a long period when the medical realm stalled and parents struggled to find any means to help their child. Many of these parents were educators, scientists, and physicians. They carefully observed their children and built cooperative networks to share experiences. Eventually, parents learned that a combination of various interventions such as diet, vitamins, behavioral modification, and specialized education was needed, specific to their own individual child. As a result, best practices in treating autism have emerged as a model of successful integrative medicine.

My New Reality

It was a typical spring day in sunny California the day it actually sunk in. The sun was shining and the birds were singing and everything appeared to be right with the world. Everything, that is, except for the unwelcomed truth I had finally and reluctantly just realized.

Could this actually be true? Is this really happening?

Time seemed to stand still and the feeling of "knowing" was my only reality. I knew this was real, I knew I was right, and I knew this was going to change my life.

I knew that Chanel had experienced a regression in her speech and social skills since that seizure, and that as the seizure activity continued, there was further delay in her development; but I never imagined that she had a serious disability that would affect her entire life.

Oh my God, Chanel has a disability...she is really NOT "going to be okay," like her dad keeps telling me.

As I stood there alone in my kitchen staring out my sliding glass door, my mind was stuck on repeated thoughts of Chanel's inability to communicate. The doctor's relentless diagnosis of autism continued to torment me and I became paralyzed with fear. Terror raced through my veins.

She really does have autism…Oh my God, what am I going to do? What is Chanel's life going to be like? Why!?! Why has this happened to my beautiful baby girl!?! Oh my God. What will her future hold?

The fear I felt for my own child was so much more powerful than any fear I've ever felt for myself. I was overwhelmed with the unknown, for our future, for the health and well-being of my precious child. Like most mothers, I would do anything to keep my child safe and to ensure that she would grow up healthy and strong. And up until that moment, I thought I was equipped to meet all her needs.

What am I going to do now? I don't know ANYTHING about raising a special needs child, and I certainly don't know ANYTHING about autism!

My body was paralyzed from head to toe. Apparently, terror and sadness had cancelled each other out and left my body with no feeling at all. As the tears streamed down my face, their warmth seemed to slowly soften my stiffened body and I began to gently shake as sobs of sorrow turned into gut-wrenching grief.

It's Up to Me

My husband did not believe it, and so I was in this alone, as are many mothers of special needs children. In fact, statistics show that dads spend more time in the denial stage than mothers. Moms will historically fall into their motherly intuition, which causes them to accept the diagnosis and move into action rather quickly. My husband, Michael, certainly was one of those dads who refused to believe for a long time. He continued to respond with comments like, "She will grow out of it and be fine. Don't worry about it. By the time she gets into Kindergarten, she will be talking—you'll see. She is only three years old—there is nothing wrong with her! Look at her! She knows exactly what we are talking about! She is the perfect child! I don't believe what the doctors are saying."

I remember looking at my big, burly husband with his brow furrowed in frustration and his dark curly hair a disheveled mess. His dark brown eyes looked both worried and determined. As I listened to his words, I wondered how this incredibly caring and loving father could be so blind. I suddenly realized that I was very alone.

Because he believed that Chanel would be fine, he could not share in my fear of what the future might bring, or understand my incessant questions and feelings of anger about how and why this happened. He did not want to talk about my doubt and confusion in my relationship with God. And so I was completely alone as the cycle of grief began for me, as it does for every parent of a special needs child.

It was up to me to find some way to help her.

I Refuse to Believe Them

I knew in my gut that I just couldn't accept or believe the grim diagnosis I had received from the doctor at UCLA. Unwilling to blindly accept the doctor's prognosis as Chanel's reality, I took her to another developmental pediatrician to get a second opinion. She was an "autism specialist" who confirmed the diagnosis and provided me with references and additional information I would need to navigate my way through the days and years ahead.

The list of therapies to research and prescriptive orders to have Chanel further tested could have been in written in Chinese as far as I was concerned. I had no idea what any of it meant, what these therapies were or any of the service providers that treat the many disorders that relate to autism.

"Occupational Therapy, Speech and Language Therapy, Applied Behavior Analysis Therapy, Play Therapy, Auditory Processing testing, Visual processing testing, PT scan, EEG..." I could almost feel my brain trying to shut down as the list went on and on. Not only did we have an autism diagnosis but also we had a comorbid diagnosis because of the seizure disorder. Little did I know that the autism was a much more clear and straightforward plan to follow. The seizure disorder would bring us years of seizure testing and searching for the right neurologist who could help us identify the medicine that would control her seizures.

The autism specialist told me the School District and Regional Center (a California State funded disability agency) would assist me in getting the help Chanel needed.

I took all of this information and guidance and went to work.

Many of you may be in this process right now. You may have just received the diagnosis and have no clue about where to begin to help your child. I've been there. It is mind-boggling. But I learned an invaluable lesson at this point. At the time, I did not know it would be invaluable, but looking back in retrospect, this is so very profound to me now: *Not all the answers you're given are right for your child.* When you receive a diagnosis, an evaluation, or even recommendations and opinions from educators, family, and friends, don't immediately accept them as truth for your child.

Do It for Your Angel

This would be a good point to begin journaling and evaluating the situations, information, recommendations, and opinions that you have received or learned from "professionals" that do not resonate with you regarding your child.

Write down all of the information, recommendations, and opinions you've heard from "professionals" (doctors, educators, etc.).

Now go back through the list and cross off all of those that simply don't resonate with you. In your gut, you know that it's wrong. Not just because you don't want to believe it, but because your instincts tell you it's not true.

In my case, I would have crossed off the words: "She'll never be verbal" and "She'll never be able to get along at school."

Now, write what you choose to continue to believe about your child.

Mine would have read, "I believe that Chanel will read, write, speak, and go to school like every other child."

You will be exposed to the opinions of friends and family and be given diagnoses from doctors and psychologists. Educators, therapists, and service providers will label your child. And many of these people will present you with their own "professional" opinion and prognosis that may include their own limiting beliefs regarding your child's future.

When something does not ring true regarding your child, "take it with a grain of salt." You are the parent and you know your child better than anyone else. You have the authority to make the ultimate decision regarding how you will move forward on the journey of assisting your child.

In other words, follow your heart.

Situations like this will come up constantly, when you will be faced with the question, "Should I take this information in, use it, apply it, and believe it to be true for my child?"

I did not believe the diagnosis that I received from the developmental pediatricians at UCLA. There was not one moment when I believed the doctor's bleak prediction to be true. I knew that Chanel would talk, read, write, and go to school like every other child.

When doctors, educators, psychologists and service providers place ceilings and limitations on children, they are robbing our children of the possibility of reaching their potential. No one has the right to predict the outcome or foretell a child's future.

Understandably, there are professional opinions, but that is all they are—opinions based upon that particular professional's knowledge and historical medical data and, therefore, a hypothesis.

Psycho-educational Assessment

It is typical for parents to be at a loss to know how to respond when they hear psychologists say things like, "Your child is functioning commensurate with their cognitive ability." I have witnessed countless students with autism who have surpassed the low expectations of IEP team members when the parent did not accept these kinds of limiting recommendations and bleak prognosis.

As I sit in hundreds of IEP meetings, year after year, I continue to hear similar kinds of limiting predictions from educators, psychologists, speech and language pathologists, and school district administrators. Standardized testing is a snapshot that provides a baseline for strengths and weakness of the student in all areas that are related to the child's disability. The problem with standardized testing is that the majority of students with autism are not successful in showing their true ability through these kinds of tests. Even the non-verbal testing cannot be relied upon to give an accurate picture of a student's true abilities. The problem this poses is the entire development of a special education program is based upon assessment findings, which determine the goals and objectives, which drive the supports and services and ultimately the placement for the child. This is why it is so important to ensure that you receive a psycho-educational assessment that focuses on the student's strengths with recommendations that outline high expectations for the child's educational future. With an assessment such as this, you, as the parent, will have the evidence you need to cause the school district to provide the goals, supports and services, and placement that your child needs to reach their potential.

If I had allowed doctor after doctor, educator after educator, and psychologist after psychologist to influence my hopes and dreams for my daughter's future, Chanel would never have graduated high school, nor would she be the self-sufficient, well-balanced, beautiful young woman she is today.

Connect with other Parents

Take care of yourself by connecting with other parents who are experiencing the same feelings that every parent of a newly diagnosed child faces. Find a support group in your area that will address your feelings of isolation, anger, and fear. This will greatly assist you in the grief process and allow you to realize that you are not alone and share common ground with many other parents who are on the same journey.

It is a typical occurrence to have your closest loved ones, friends and family, find it extremely difficult to support us in our time of need. It is a scary place to go—the world of disability. But if you can share these feelings with other parents who are experiencing the same challenges, you will fill the void of isolation. We are not alone. There are thousands of other families facing the same issues every day. Walking with others in tunnels of darkness opens us up for the light to come in so we can see where we are going. The best thing that you can do is provide yourself with emotional support and connection.

A Recipe for Anger

I continued to follow my heart and use my parental intuition as my guide, but I still faced challenges that I now know most parents of special needs children face, even twenty years later.

First, I found myself in a whole new universe called autism, which I knew nothing about. And, as I've already shared, as I began to gather information from doctors, educators, and my own research, I was faced with the constant question, *Who should I trust and believe, and is this information what is right for my child?*

Second, I found myself in many situations in which I felt judged by other people's opinions and their lack of knowledge and awareness about autism. Autism, and autistic-like behaviors, can produce fear and feelings of discomfort in people who don't understand it, which can challenge relationships and cause feelings of isolation. Feelings of abandonment by my friends, family, and church members, also added to my fear of drowning in my confusion. For many years, I felt like no one understood Chanel or me. (Even my husband didn't get it!) And because I was so busy taking care of my angel and trying to navigate the system and manage my emotions, I didn't really have the time, energy, or patience to try and explain what I was dealing with in an attempt to maintain relationships. When I did have those uncomfortable conversations, the outcome would only fuel my frustration because I would be confronted with denial, anger, or even judgment.

Left Out

It was common for Chanel to not be invited to birthday parties and play dates that were happening all around us. For some reason, there seemed to be some unspoken agreement or understanding that Chanel wasn't included in the social events going on for the kids. Whether it was friends from school, church, neighbors, or within our own family, Chanel was not invited. The problem was that I never got the memo and never agreed to this treatment of my child. I would be having a discussion with friends or family and the conversation would switch to the upcoming party or social event and they would have no awareness of how hurt I was because Chanel was left out again. Year after year, the kids would be right outside playing in the street, but there would never be a knock on the door to invite her to come out and play.

This is the story of hundreds of thousands of parents of children with special needs.

We are required to facilitate friendships and ask parents if they would be willing to have their typical child come and play with our kids. If parents of typical children don't encourage their kids to play with the special kids, this won't change. If typical kids are going to be successful in developing friendships with our kids, they must be given the information they need to understand that special needs children may not talk well or be able to keep up with the games that they play, but they are children too and enjoy many of the same things that typical children do.

On the other hand, the friends Chanel made at school in her general education classrooms were invited to come to Chanel's birthday party every year (and they did come, year after year). They were all very sweet and they did honestly care about Chanel after being in school with her for many years. I believe that Chanel was invited to two parties during her six years in grade school, and those two parties were the happiest days of our lives. We were so excited when Chanel got those invitations to come to a party from a typical friend. It was like a dream come true!

There is a huge difference between *saying* you love or care about a child and *teaching* your children to treat them the same way they would treat any other friend. Being an example of unconditional love by including kids who appear to be different does not come naturally to children, it needs to be taught and modeled to them by their parents.

My other kids have all profoundly internalized this lesson of inclusion by growing up with Chanel. As children and now as adults, when they see a special needs individual, no matter the disability, they treat them with respect, speak to them without hesitation, and will stand up for them if need be, without questioning whether it should be any other way.

Much of this can be attributed to the fact that special needs children are not included in general education classes, so how can typical developing children learn to include them in their play during school and outside of school? As inclusion increases and parents begin to teach their children about tolerance and acceptance, we can all make a difference in the lives of these children. All children benefit from learning the invaluable life lesson that even though we may appear to have differences, we are really all the same. We all just want to be loved unconditionally, and this is the message that our kids are here to teach us.

The stress of being in new territory and unfamiliar with the language of a bureaucratic system coupled with the feelings of isolation from my friends, family, and church community as well as the "experts" who should be helping our kids, truly becomes a recipe for deep frustration, anger, and resentment.

I was on a collision course with some of the most intense emotion I would ever experience.

*"The highest, most decisive experience
is to be alone with one's own self.
You must be alone to find out what supports you,
when you find that you cannot support yourself.
Only this experience can give you an
indestructible foundation."*

C.G. Jung

CHAPTER 2

CHARIOTS OF FURY

I was looking through the clothes rack, trying to find my size, while Chanel was verbalizing her typical video talk—repeating a phrase, over and over again, from one of her favorite movies with the same exact tone and inflection used in the movie.

"I knew that was you!" a familiar voice piped from behind me.

"Lisa!" We hugged, sharing our joy in running into each other.

"I heard Chanel video talking from across the store. The closer I got, I knew it was her!" Lisa chuckled and I couldn't help but giggle. "You know, Valerie, us 'moms of autistic children' can spot another autistic child a mile away."

We talked and talked, like we always did, and finally realized we better pause the conversation and get home. It was always that way with Lisa. I could talk to her for hours and still find more things to talk about. I was so comfortable with her and trusted her enough to share anything and everything that was going on in my life and how I felt about it, especially when it came to matters of parenting an autistic angel. We attended the same church every Sunday and our husbands were good friends, so we would have a great time together as couples going to church, out to dinner, and just hanging out together. She was just one of those friends during a time when those friendships were hard to come by, and I cherished our relationship and everything she taught me about advocating for my angel. In fact, Lisa was the first person to introduce me to parental rights and opened the door for my advocacy journey when

Chanel was newly diagnosed and I was clueless about what she needed.

Lisa lived in my neighborhood with her autistic son who was the same age as Chanel. We met when our kids were four years old, and he was attending a special school for students with autism on the school district's dime—a special, non-public school that provided intensive intervention, which included all of the supports and services a child on the autism spectrum requires.

I quickly learned that Chanel was not being provided what she needed and became determined to have her placed at the same school Lisa's son was attending. She carefully guided me through the process of learning my parental rights and how to advocate for Chanel, who was only five years old when I experienced that first big "win."

At this non-public school, she received Speech and Language Therapy, Occupational Therapy, ABA, Auditory Integration Therapy, and specialized teaching strategies that a child with autistic-like behaviors requires. She improved so much while attending this pre-school that when she was ready to come back into our local public school, she did not present as a typical autistic child. She was very compliant and exhibited very typical behavior for a child of six years, but she was still non-verbal.

Following my heart about the type of intensive early intervention she needed was paying off in a big way, but there was more work to do.

Early Intervention

Research shows that the earlier an autistic child receives care, the better his or her prospects for living an independent and productive life become. Doctors tell us that providing intensive early intervention during the window of time when the child's brain and cognitive systems are in their first stages of development is extremely important. The "wait and see" approach forfeits that window of time forever.

The American Academy of Pediatrics recommends screening for autism at 18 and 24 month check-ups, simply to reinforce the idea that autism, when caught early, can be treated even more effectively. For all of the advancements we have made in the past few decades, for all of the science that has helped revolutionize treatment, nothing can replace early intervention as the most effective step that a parent can take.

After eighteen months of this specialized program, Chanel was ready to come back to our local school district for first grade. It was then that I realized the plight that every parent faces in meeting the educational needs of their special needs child. The local school district did not offer a program that was even close to the intensive intervention that she had received in the non-public school, and the Individualized Education Plan (IEP) team meetings were not designed to help the parent or the child.

It was a rude awakening to the special education system and the fight that was about to ensue. Although I didn't know it at the time, experiencing anger was the next phase in moving through the cycle of grief. How could I not feel angry? I was faced with so many unanswered questions, and many times I felt so alone, so afraid, and so angry as I fought to help Chanel find her wings.

My feelings of fear and anger fueled me to take action. I kept following my heart and learning. It was all I could do.

Fighting for Inclusion

"Mr. and Mrs. Aprahamian, the district's offer of Free and Appropriate Public Education (FAPE) is to place Chanel in a Severely Handicapped, Special Day Class (SH SDC), which is a special education classroom, with other students who have been diagnosed with autism." The district administrator's voice was monotone and matter-of-fact as if she had memorized her lines for the meeting. As I sat across the large conference room table, I watched as the heads of the teacher, school psychologist, several other school district staff members and service providers all seem to nod in unison, as if they had performed this ritual a million times before.

I felt my insides begin to tremble with both fear and anger and quickly averted my eyes to collect myself. *Valerie, hold it together. Chanel needs you to stay calm and fight for what's best for her.* Pulling my gaze back from the bare walls, stacks of files, and a giant ticking clock, I calmly clasped my hands on the large wooden conference table in front of me and forced a smile at the twelve pairs of eyes peering in my direction.

"I'm sorry, but my husband and I do not agree with that approach. We are requesting that Chanel be included in a general education classroom with special education supports and services to give her access to the general education curriculum." In just one year, I had done a lot of research about the school system and my parental rights with Lisa's guidance. She had encouraged me to go into my first IEP meeting armed with information and determination.

Least Restrictive Environment

Inclusion means educating a student with a disability in the Least Restrictive Environment (LRE), or in other words, the most appropriate placement as close to a typical general education classroom possible.

Statistics show that educating a student with special needs along with their typical developing peers is the most effective education. This model not only benefits the special needs student but also enhances and enriches the classroom experience for the typical developing child in the general education classroom.

If a child is segregated with other students who have the same deficits in which they model atypical behavior, the student will most likely make very little progress. Yet, when a special needs student is placed in a class that allows the child to model typical behavior and social skills, most children will ultimately model that same appropriate behavior.

The frowns and furrowed eyebrows of the IEP team revealed their frustration with my challenge of their recommendation for Chanel.

And so the debate began…

The district administrator responded tersely with her rote rebuttal, "Mr. and Mrs. Aprahamian, your daughter does not have the skills or test scores to support your request. She is *not* ready to be placed in a general education classroom. The team does not feel that a regular classroom is the appropriate placement for your daughter."

"I understand that. But the Individuals Disability Education Act (IDEA) states that a child is not required to be placed in a general education class," I responded, albeit with a little tremor to my voice.

IDEA (Individuals Disabilities Education Act)

"Federal law under IDEA" (Individuals Disabilities Education Act) states that a child should not be placed outside the general education classroom unless all appropriate supports and services are provided. If the child is not successful in receiving educational benefit by accessing the general education curriculum after all appropriate supports and services have been provided to the child, then and only then, the child may be placed in an alternative placement other than general education class.

Their eyes widened. I clearly knew more than most of the parents they misinformed in these meetings, and I made sure they knew it with my next comment: "Plus,

Chanel does not exhibit disruptive, self-stimulation, or maladaptive behaviors."

More on Behaviors

Self-stimulation, stemming, or maladaptive behaviors are actions or movements that autistic children exhibit when they need to self-sooth and regulate themselves when they are sensory overloaded or become anxious in challenging situations. It can look like hand-flapping, rocking, pacing back and forth, waving their fingers in front of their eyes, or just repeating an action or verbalization over and over again. Many children with autistic-like behaviors will exhibit some kind of stemming or perseverative behaviors.

The energy in the room was hostile and their faces were somber and serious. I had already learned that the district facilitated IEP's in this manner in an attempt to intimidate or coerce parents into agreeing with the school district's agenda for the child.

"With all due respect, I'm not going to settle for this recommendation when I *know* my daughter could handle a regular classroom with the appropriate supports and services."

This was the mid-1990s, and I was appalled at the injustice of it all. I could not believe that it was common practice for school districts to disregard and disrespect parental rights. Shocked at the indifference of district staff members in the way they interacted with me and some of the parents I was beginning to meet, I witnessed them using tactics that antagonized, alienated, and intimidated parents—behaviors that completely oppose the principles and aspirations of the IEP meeting according to IDEA.

The purpose of an IEP meeting is to ensure that the special needs child's educational needs are met according to State and Federal law. But in reality, the IEP meeting was being used as a platform to negotiate bureaucratic power plays based on funding issues and the ego of the administrator who held the authority to incorporate their own agenda and dictate the outcome of the meeting.

The school district thought I was crazy and tried to convince me that Chanel needed to be placed in a severely handicapped autism classroom. My request for inclusion was very unusual at that time, but I had a knowing that it was right for Chanel. I was unmovable in my decision, and I would not allow anything to detour my conviction.

Year after year at every annual IEP meeting, the district would attempt to place Chanel in a special education classroom. And year after year, I remained steadfast to my conviction that Chanel should be fully included in the general education classroom, until she was in high school. By that time, she had acquired the skills necessary to access the general education curriculum, which allowed her to remain on a diploma track. In high school, Chanel was placed in a non-severe special education classroom, which provided the accommodations and modifications she needed to be successful in accessing the general education curriculum to graduate with a diploma.

Today, Chanel can communicate very well and has great social skills. Many people don't even realize she has the diagnosis of autism until they have had a lengthy conversation with her. You could not pick Chanel out of a group of peers because she does not look or act like a young adult with autism because throughout elementary and intermediate school, she was never segregated with other students with autism or placed in a special needs class that would allow her to model those kinds of behaviors and characteristics. Instead, Chanel was given the opportunity to learn typical behavior and aspire to the expectations equal to that of a typical child.

Inclusion

When I advocated educating Chanel in the general education classroom in 1997, she was the only student with autism that was *"fully included"* in the general education classroom in my local school district. She received Resource Support for two hours a day, which is instruction in a classroom with a small amount of students, taught by a special education teacher that provides remediation and tutoring. In addition, she also received ABA (Applied Behavior Analysis), Occupational Therapy and Speech and Language Therapy and worked with an academic tutor after school.

Looking back and knowing what I know now about "Full-Inclusion," there is so much I did not know then that I could have done differently. In addition, school districts were also just beginning to learn how to include a student on the spectrum in a general education classroom. Nevertheless, the fact that Chanel was able to be educated with her typical developing peers was unprecedented at the time. The only reason I had the knowledge and awareness to demand inclusion for my daughter was because I had attended a TASH (The Association for Persons with Severe Handicaps) conference, which opened the door for me to begin researching inclusion.

According to TASH, an international advocacy association of people with disabilities, "Students with disabilities have a right to be educated in the regular education classroom with their non-disabled peers. Education in regular education settings implies more than just physical presence; it includes access to the curriculum that is taught in the regular education classroom."

TASH advocates that "Students with disabilities are entitled under the Fourteenth Amendment of the U.S. Constitution, federal civil rights law, including Section 504 of the Rehabilitation Act of 1973, the Individuals with Disabilities Education Act, and the Americans with Disabilities Act, their respective state constitutions, and state law, to be free from discrimination and to be provided equal educational opportunity to learn what all other students are expected to learn. Indeed, the IDEA, Section 504, and the ADA all require, as they have from their inception, that students with disabilities must be educated in regular education settings to the maximum extent appropriate in light of their needs, and prohibit their exclusion unless education there cannot be achieved satisfactorily even with appropriate supplementary aids and services. A school district proposing to remove a child from the regular education classroom has the burden of proving that such removal—whether partial or total—is necessary because education cannot be reasonably accomplished with the use of supplementary aids and services and/or modifications to the regular education curriculum."

Despite clear legal rights and numerous judicial rulings, students with disabilities continue to be isolated and separately educated, provided a diluted and inferior education, and denied meaningful opportunities to learn. As recently as 1997, the United States Congress in reauthorizing and amending the Individuals with Disabilities Education Act, admitted in findings codified at 20 U.S.C. 1400(b)(4) that: '...implementation of this Act has been impeded by low expectations, and an insufficient focus on applying replicable research on proven methods of teaching and learning for children with disabilities...' This, in spite of more than 20 years of research and experience providing evidence that the 'education of children with disabilities can be made more effective by having high expectations for such children and ensuring their access to the general curriculum to the maximum extent possible.' 20 U.S.C. 1400(c)(4).

"Because of this long history of exclusion and discrimination, many students with disabilities have been denied access to the general education curriculum, excluded from the school they would attend if not for their disability, and unnecessarily isolated from their age appropriate peers who are not disabled."

"To achieve such an education, support services must be provided as needed, programs and curricula must be modified as needed, and students must receive such supports, supplementary aids and services as are necessary in an inclusive setting. The expectation shall be that every school community shall provide a quality, inclusive education for all students with disabilities that is predicated on a shared vision of high expectations for all students and a commitment to a set of learning goals or standards that are strong, clear, understood, and put into practice."

"Local, state, provincial, regional and federal governments, as well as all related organizations, stand accountable for the development and maintenance of educational opportunities for all students that are inclusive and ultimately effective. All governments must be urged to enforce vigorously, at all levels, legislation that assures quality, inclusive educational practices."

It has been eighteen years since I first advocated for Chanel to be placed in a general education class, and a lot has changed.

First, autism prevalence as reported in the scientific literature increased by more than 600% from 1989-2009. In fact, the most recent numbers are 1 in every 68 children being born on the autism spectrum. Ten years ago, autism's estimated prevalence was 1 in 166. Today it's 1 in 68—an increase of more than 100% in one decade. Therefore, placing students with autism in a segregated classroom is no longer a viable or effective option, in spite of the fact that there is still so much fear and resistance from general education teachers and parents of typical developing students regarding inclusion. At the rate of newly diagnosed children, what are we going to do with the increasing numbers of autistic students five years from now? Second, the inclusion model has evolved into providing many supports and services *within* the classroom instead of pulling the student out of the classroom in order to receive services.

It is my opinion that although we have progressed in thinking inclusively, we have a long way to go in terms of teaching general education teachers to accept and allow service providers to "push-in" to the general and special education classrooms. Many general education teachers feel it is not their job to educate a special needs child. Others do a beautiful job at including students on IEP's as an equal member of the classroom.

An IEP is a team approach. It is not possible, nor is it appropriate, to expect a general education teacher to meet the needs of a special needs child without the support of additional special education teachers and service providers. Inclusion really works when the IEP members work as a cohesive team to support one another in order to meet the needs of the child. For students to access the general education curriculum, accommodations and most likely, modifications of curriculum are essential. The special education teacher is a key player in supporting the general education teacher to implement the appropriate modifications of the general education curriculum.

By now, most of humanity knows that we are facing the challenge of how to meet the needs of the increasing numbers of autistic children coming into our world every day. As families, educational systems, health care providers, and society in general continue to struggle with making the changes necessary to accommodate this population, we must ask ourselves, "What is the lesson we can learn from this profound evolutionary process that continues to grow exponentially year after year?"

Do It For Your Angel

It's time to take out your journal and answer some questions: 1) What was your experience at the last IEP meeting? 2) What are the placement and support services your child is currently being provided? 3) Have you considered the Least Restrictive Placement for your child? 4) Have all appropriate accommodations been identified? 5) If you feel your child is in the correct placement, is the academic curriculum being modified appropriately with measurable goals and objectives? 6) Looking at the list of placement options below, which one seems like the best fit for your child?

Special Education Placement
A Continuum of Placement Options

General Education Placement
The first and most least restrictive environment is of course general education.

Resource Support Placement (RSP)

The next would be a Resource Support Classroom, which is a classroom that is taught by a special education teacher with a smaller class size. The child is pulled from General Education to go to RSP to receive "tutoring" in the subject areas that the student needs support and remediation.

Special Education Classroom (SDC)

The next more restrictive placement would be a Special Education Classroom or Special Day Class (SDC). This class is taught by a special education teacher and the child usually attends for a full day unless they go to a general education class for a strong subject area or elective. A Special Day Class provides the same standardized general education curriculum equal to that of a General Education class with the accommodations and modifications as necessary.

Severely Handicapped Special Day Class (SH SDC)

The even more restrictive placement would be a Severely Handicapped Special Day Class (SH SDC), which is a classroom that is taught by a special education teacher. It would depend upon the student whether this student would take part with other students during lunch, recess, or Physical Education. Most of these students that are in a severely handicapped program are not with typical students at all for the entire school day. The Severely Handicapped Class is not mandated to teach general education curriculum but instead will focus on the functional goals of the student.

Many students are misplaced in SH classrooms and, as a result, regress in the academic achievement they received prior to that placement. It is common for parents to tell me how unhappy they are with their child's placement, explaining, "My child was doing math and reading fine until they were placed in an SH program. Now, my child has forgotten how to do math or read and can't even write a paragraph. When I ask the teacher when they work on Math, she states that they only work on money skills and that they only learn to read community signs and memorize their personal information so they can repeat it or write it down."

If you don't want to be one of these parents, it is imperative to learn the continuum of placements for special education in order to ensure that your child is placed in the most least restrictive environment in order for them to receive the educational benefit they deserve.

I am not advocating that general education would be appropriate or effective for every special needs student. I am simply stating that the LRE must be considered very carefully. If the student has not been provided with the opportunity to receive every appropriate support and service that is available under IDEA, placing a child outside the general education classroom might be premature.

Under the Surface

All parents of a newly diagnosed child are faced with many unanswered questions: "Why did this happen to my child? What can I do to help them? Why is it so hard to get them the support they need?" We are constantly presented with difficult decisions that we feel unequipped to make. "What kind of classroom does my child need? What type of therapy will really help them? What are my parental rights?" Every day, we are reminded of our child's unknown future and wonder how the disability will affect the rest of their lives. "What if I can't get my child what they need from the school district? What if I can't get the district to listen to me?"

All of these questions shake our foundation, and can make us feel incredibly isolated and out of control. Who could possibly understand the frustration and pressure we are feeling? Who could possibly grasp what it's like to raise an angel with these types of needs? Who could possibly empathize with this situation when they are raising typical children and worrying about typical things? We can quickly begin to feel fear that escalates into anger, especially when it feels as though we are powerless to help and protect our children.

To add to our unanswered questions, we are faced with the emotions of the grief cycle. The first reaction is shock, denial, confusion and often a sense of abandonment by family and friends. We may not know it at the time, but the initial overriding emotion is actually loss—the loss of the dreams and expectations of what we had envisioned for our child and for our family.

As the loss sets in, we find ourselves in an overwhelming new world of information in which we have no idea how to navigate. Soon, we are seeing doctors, therapists, and specialists. Immediately, we are connected with government disability agencies and special education administrators without the knowledge of what to ask for or what is even appropriate for our child. Our lack of knowledge leaves us at the mercy of these agencies, trusting that they will do what is right for our child. Eventually, we learn that their system cannot be trusted because decisions are based upon funding, power plays, and a bureaucratic agenda.

It's a recipe for anger...

Bus Ride Terror

"Michael, Chanel is not home from the bus yet and she should have been here twenty-five minutes ago," I said as a daunting feeling in my stomach began to grow.

"I know, Honey. Let's call the school district and see what's going on," Michael replied calmly.

"Hello, yes, this is Valerie Aprahamian and Chanel's bus is twenty-five minutes late. Do you have any information about that route or what is going on?"

"Let me look into it and give you a call back, Mrs. Aprahamian," the district secretary replied without any concern.

Chanel was six years old at the time. She was still non-verbal and could not talk at all. She couldn't state her name much less recite her address or phone number, and my mind began to work against me. *What if there was an accident? Where is she? Why haven't they returned our call yet?* I tried to remain calm but my motherly instincts were beginning to scream.

Twenty minutes went by and now I was worried. I called again. "Yes, this is Mrs. Aprahamian again. Where is the bus? Where is my daughter?"

"Well, there seems to be a problem with the two-way radio, Mrs. Aprahamian. We can't seem to reach the bus driver so they must be in an area where the radios don't work." The secretary seemed unsure and evasive about her information, yet continued to try and diminish the urgency of the situation. Her attempts to placate me made me angry.

"What do you mean, you can't reach the bus driver? What is being done about this? I need some answers, and I need them now."

"We are trying to reach the driver and will let you know as soon as we have some information for you, Mrs. Aprahamian."

If she says my name to calm me down one more time... My panic transformed into terrified rage, my hands trembling as I slammed the phone down on the kitchen counter.

I began pacing in circles and praying, "Please, Lord, take care of Chanel. Send her angels to watch over her. Please keep her safe. Please bring her home."

Another fifteen minutes had passed and still no call. The bus was now more than an hour late.

My husband called this time. "Have you reached the bus driver? Where is our daughter?!?" Fear and fury surged through his voice.

"I don't know how to tell you this, Mr. Aprahamian, but we cannot reach the bus driver and we do not know where the bus is. The other children on that route were dropped off at their homes and we don't understand why Chanel has not been dropped off yet. There is a substitute bus driver on that route today, and she is unfamiliar with the route."

"What the hell are you talking about, lady? I want to talk to the director immediately! If my daughter is not home within five minutes, I am calling the police."

"Calm down, Mr. Aprahamian. I don't appreciate being yelled at. I am doing everything I can. We will let you know as soon as we receive more information."

"Oh really! Well you have not called us back once yet! I want to speak to someone in control right now!"

The secretary would not allow us to speak to anyone else, even though we knew the administrators and transportation department were there in the office trying to locate the bus and Chanel.

Ninety minutes had passed and I was beside myself. *Has this bus driver kidnapped Chanel? She is the only child left on the bus! She is alone with a substitute bus driver. Who is this person? How long has she been working for the district? What is she doing with my daughter? Chanel can't talk! Oh my God! Where is she?*

I stood over the kitchen sink, feeling as though I might throw up. Michael was yelling and screaming, and I started to cry. Desperation and utter helplessness overcame me. There was nothing we could do but wait.

"That's it. I'm calling the police." Michael picked up the phone and reported what was going on, but slammed it down again when they told him there was nothing they could do until more time had passed.

After what seemed an eternity, the secretary called, stating that the bus driver had taken Chanel to our previous address—to a home where we hadn't lived for over a year. She said the parents who answered the door stated that Chanel didn't live there and that she had made all her other pick-ups from several other schools on her route and dropped off all the other children at their homes, and then taken Chanel back to the old address once again. This was the reason for the two hours that had passed.

Another thirty minutes went by and Chanel still was missing when the secretary called again. "The bus is outside your house." We went outside and there was no bus.

By this time, we were completely at our wits' end and screaming at the secretary. "The bus is not here! Where is she? The bus is not in front of our house!"

The secretary finally figured out that the bus driver had taken Chanel back to our old address a second time and was sitting in front of it.

"Tell that bus driver not to move or take our daughter anywhere else! We are on our way to pick her up right now! Do not let that driver move!"

We frantically drove to our previous home, which was less than ten minutes away. When we pulled up, a total of three hours had passed without our sweet baby girl safely in our arms.

"Where in the hell have you been with our daughter?" I yelled at the bus driver, who looked homeless with missing teeth, pockmarks, and grime on her face and hair. I was horrified.

"I had the wrong address," she mumbled.

"Why didn't you contact the district office as soon as you realized you didn't have the correct address and my daughter couldn't tell you where she lived? How could you take every other child home and leave my poor daughter sitting on the bus terrified and alone? What is wrong with you?" I couldn't keep my tone from rising with fury.

I scooped up Chanel, noticing her soiled state. *Three hours is a stretch for her bladder and she must have been scared out of her mind.* Trembling, I got into our car with Chanel, and slammed the car door.

Relieved and grateful to have her back in my arms safely, I was still burning with anger at the incompetence of the district as they handled the entire situation. *I can't believe that a special education administrator did not once get on the phone with me at some point and that secretary was actually upset because we were yelling at her! She was more worried about defending her ego than she was about the safety and well-being of our precious child!*

The fire of anger continued to expand inside my stomach, and I bit my tongue to keep from screaming all the way home. *My poor Chanel Lee...I have to hold it together and remain calm for her and just get her home.*

Needless to say, my daughter never rode the bus again. I called the special education administrators to discuss the situation. Essentially, they put the blame on the transportation department. I called the transportation department and they took no responsibility for the incident either. No one apologized or took ownership for what had occurred, but they did implement a policy to have all non-verbal children riding buses wear a nametag which identified their address, telephone number, and parents' names.

To top it all off, I had a meeting with the SELPA Director to discuss Chanel's support services shortly after the bus incident. During the meeting, I brought up how disappointed I was with the outcome of the investigation and voiced my frustration regarding the fact that no one was willing to take responsibility for putting my child in danger. The SELPA Director's response was, "If I have to hear about this bus incident one more time, I think I will die."

My fury at the system was growing, and over the years, there were plenty of situations that intensified it.

Do It For Your Angel

Take out your journal and write down all of the major problems or situations you have faced with the system. How could these incidents have been avoided? What can you do to prevent something like this from happening again in the future? In my case, I made a list of the administrators, teachers, and staff members and their direct contact information and began to document all communication regarding Chanel in writing through emails or letters. I also began to research the complaint process to address the inadequate outcome of the bus investigation. I now know that there is a powerful process that parents can utilize to hold districts accountable. This is the Uniform Complaint, which is at the district level and the Compliance Complaint, which is at the State level. Parents can also file a complaint with the Office of Civil Rights.

Camp Lies

It was late afternoon and my husband and I were anxious about how Chanel was doing on the school camping trip. It was the custom of my local school district for 6th graders to attend science camp in Lake Arrowhead with their class. This was an event that students and parents talked about and looked forward to and now, Chanel was actually going too!

She should have arrived in Arrowhead by now and the kids are probably getting settled into their rooms. I hope Chanel is okay and having fun! Her teacher (we will call her "Mrs. Underwood" for confidentiality purposes) *gave me her word that she would take care of Chanel. You have to learn to trust, Valerie!*

I dismissed the worry, trying to think positively and hold on to the hope that Chanel would be successful in taking part in an event that all the "typical" kids experience as 6th graders. There had been so many events in which Chanel was not included because of her autism and seizure disorder. *This is going to be different. Chanel will remember this for the rest of her life. She got to go to science camp with all of her childhood friends!*

My tummy fluttered with feelings of anxiety and celebration.

Just as I was getting myself settled, the phone rang. "Mrs. Aprahamian, this is the medic at camp. Chanel has had a seizure and we would like to know what you want us to do."

"Oh my God, is she still seizing? Did you call 911? Do you have the Medical Health Action Plan?"

"I am not aware of a medical plan, but she is in another cabin. I don't know if they have called 911. They just asked that I call you and let you know," the man answered hesitantly.

"Well can you please have her teacher or someone who is with her call me back immediately? And if she is still seizing, 911 should be called immediately!" That familiar burning knot in my stomach reappeared and my body stiffened with fear.

A few minutes later, the medic called us back. "Chanel is in the medic office and she is not seizing any longer. She seems very tired and is sleeping."

Chanel's teacher got on the phone. "Mrs. Aprahamian, Chanel is fine. She is resting and her vitals are normal and she will be fine. Please don't worry."

"What happened, Mrs. Underwood?" I needed details about the seizure. "How long did it last and when did it happen?" I didn't try to hide my impatience.

"After we arrived at camp, the kids decided to take a little hike nearby and Chanel had a seizure," she replied, failing to answer my questions.

"Were you there with her, Mrs. Underwood?" I had a horrible feeling that she wasn't being forthcoming with me. *Why isn't she just telling me what I need to hear? I need details!*

"No, I stayed back at camp. I wasn't there so I really don't know exactly what happened, but I can assure you that she is fine."

My blood began to boil. *I can't believe this. Mrs. Underwood promised me she would be with Chanel every minute and that she would be safe. She broke her promise and they haven't even been there for three hours!*

"We're driving up to get her."

"Please don't come, Mrs. Aprahamian. She will be fine. Let her stay and enjoy the camp," she pleaded with me.

Are you kidding me? How can I trust you to keep my daughter safe when you broke your promise as soon as you arrived?

"We will see you in a few hours, Mrs. Underwood."

She continued to appeal to me, mother to mother, "Valerie, please don't pick her up. Let her stay and learn that she can get through these things on her own. I promise you, she will be fine."

"We are leaving now, Mrs. Underwood." I hung up the phone and looked at my husband, whose eyes were wide with anger. "Can you believe this, Michael?"

"Yes, of course I can believe it, Valerie! Are you even surprised that they broke their promise and didn't do what they were suppose to do?"

My heart was broken with sadness and betrayal once again. I had trusted Mrs. Underwood and she let me down. But, most importantly, she let Chanel down.

It took us less than two hours to get to camp, and I was determined to get the true facts of the event. We went straight to Chanel in the medic office and found her resting, which was normal after a seizure.

I turned to face the medic, some other camp staff members, and Mrs. Underwood. "Where was Chanel when this seizure happened?" I asked as I leaned back against the counter.

"They were taking a little hike in the woods," Mrs. Underwood answered.

"Who was with her?" I pressed.

"There were two camp employees with the group. It is our policy to have one camp counselor in the front of the line and one in the back." She was having trouble making eye contact with me.

"Then what happened?" I kept digging. *Why do I have to squeeze the information out of these people?* It was obvious they weren't willing to share details. I had the same feeling I got when I spoke to Mrs. Underwood on the phone.

My gut was telling me there was more to the story and that they were covering something up, but I was so exhausted by the intensity and anxiety of the situation that I just wanted to get Chanel home. She was safe and that's all I cared about at that moment.

Here it is again, Parents!

Listen to your parental instincts. If we listen to our intuition, we know much more than our minds can tell us. It all comes back to "Follow Your Heart."

The drive home was somber, but I put on a happy face for Chanel.

I wrote a letter to the district, stating that Chanel's IEP and medical plan was not followed properly and since the camp administrators and Chanel's teacher were not forthcoming in answering my questions about the details of Chanel's seizure, I requested an investigation and incident report to gain reliable facts surrounding the event.

At this time, Chanel had a one-on-one aide who assisted her with her academics as well as provided support in the event of a seizure, but Mrs. Underwood asked that I consider allowing Chanel to attend camp without the aide. My gut reaction was, *"Absolutely not!"* I told her I wanted someone with Chanel at all times in the event of a seizure, and she reassured me that Chanel would never be left alone. As camp approached, we had many discussions about this, and I did not come to my decision easily. My motherly instincts told me that this was not a good idea.

I wanted to trust Mrs. Underwood. I did believe that she cared for Chanel and really enjoyed having her in her general education classroom. She was one of the few general education teachers that did not complain or show concern about having Chanel in class. So I stepped out in faith and trusted Mrs. Underwood in caring for my precious angel...in spite of my own instincts and intuition telling me otherwise.

I was, however, thorough in legally preparing for Chanel to attend the camping trip. As an advocate, I knew that everything had to be documented properly in order for agreements to be defined and implemented. Prior to the trip, I called an IEP meeting with Chanel's entire IEP team to review her medical plan and ensure that everyone was on the same page in the event of a seizure. The district nurse was in attendance and, at my request, we reviewed and amended the medical plan with a fine-toothed comb.

This IEP meeting lasted for 2 hours and all team members understood the Medical Health Action Plan and how it would be implemented in the event of a seizure while Chanel was at camp. I even asked that the IEP state that the Health Plan would be provided and reviewed with the Camp Administrator and, of course, the medic.

I was assured that this would be done and the school site administrator, along with Mrs. Underwood, stated that they felt comfortable in the fidelity of this plan.

Medical Health Action Plans

When a student on an IEP has a medical issue, the district is mandated to develop what is called a "Medical Health Action Plan" which delineates the student's health issues, medications, and plan of action if the student were to have a medical issue occur during school hours. For Chanel, in the event of a seizure, a very specific plan was in place so that there was no room for error, as she continued to experience regular seizure activity.

The Medical Health Action Plan was outlined under the direction of specific doctor's recommendations, as Chanel's seizure disorder is life-threatening. Many of her seizures occurred on a weekly basis but stopped on their own after 5 minutes, while others escalated into a seizure that would not stop unless paramedics were called and medication and oxygen were administered. These seizures can cause death, brain and central nervous system damage and possible pulmonary edema if appropriate treatment is not given.

Since Chanel's initial seizure at 22 months, she has experienced every form of seizure. Statistics show that one-third of children with autism are also diagnosed with a seizure disorder. A brief summary of each type of seizure follows:

• *Tonic-clonic seizures* are the most common. Also known as *gran mal* seizures, they produce muscle stiffening followed by jerking. Gran mal seizures also produce loss of consciousness.

- *Absence seizures* can be difficult to recognize. Also known as *petit mal* seizures, they are marked by periods of unresponsiveness. The person may stare into space. He or she may or may not exhibit jerking or twitching.

- *Tonic seizures* involve muscle stiffening alone.

- *Clonic seizures* involve repeated jerking movements on both sides of the body.

- *Myoclonic seizures* involve jerking or twitching of the upper body, arms or legs.

- *Atonic seizures* involve sudden limpness, or loss of muscle tone. The person may fall or drop his or her head involuntarily.

As a result of my request for an investigation, an IEP was called to review the findings of the investigation, which were nothing short of shocking.

The truth of the facts of the incident went something like this:

After the kids arrived at camp, they got situated in their assigned cabins and then two camp counselors supervised a hike in the woods around the campgrounds. The report stated that the kids did their "count off," which was protocol for leaving the campgrounds, and were given directions to remain in a line with one counselor in the lead and another supervising from the rear. Upon returning to camp, the kids were again instructed to "count off." Chanel was missing. They could not tell me how long it took for the counselors to find Chanel after they retraced their steps back into the woods where they found Chanel seizing on the forest ground. They could not be clear regarding how much time passed before they got Chanel into the medic's office or what had transpired before I finally received the phone call.

They could not give me clear answers regarding why no one saw Chanel seizing on the ground or when she went missing from the line during the hike. They didn't call 911, which was a stated requirement for a 5+ minutes seizure in the Medical Health Action Plan. And, of course, Mrs. Underwood was not there and had not given the two counselors the information regarding Chanel's epilepsy or the procedure to follow in the event that she were to have a seizure. Mrs. Underwood could not explain why or how this happened. She was evasive in her responses to my questions regarding her sincere promises to supervise Chanel at all times, and she was authentically remorseful and very uncomfortable while the findings of the investigation were reviewed.

It took everything within me to harness my outrage and disgust at the lack of accountability of the camp administrator and school district staff.

Once again, my trust and faith in the system was betrayed. I was overcome with immense disappointment with the incompetence of everyone involved. And I was enraged that despite the fact that I took every precautionary measure as a mother and advocate, my efforts were completely disregarded and ignored. It was almost too much anger to handle.

Do It for Your Angel

Grab your journal and get all of that anger down on the page. Write down what you really think about the people you've entrusted with your child and all of the problems and ugliness you've experienced in the broken system.

I made the decision never to allow Chanel to be without an aide in order to ensure her safety and well-being. I also made a commitment to myself to always go with my gut (motherly instinct) no matter what.

What are your stories about your child? Who are you upset with?

It's okay to feel the anger. In fact, it's important to express your anger in a healthy way, and then replace it with the feelings that will help you help your child.

To move from anger to better feelings, try this exercise: Stop what you're doing and take three deep breaths. Close your eyes go inward, into your heart. Keep breathing, taking long, deep inhales through your nose and long deep exhales out your nose. Bring your awareness to the middle of your head, right behind your eyes. Keep breathing. This will bring you into the present moment, where you will begin to feel the fear and anger dissipate and leave your body. Now you have some space open for feelings of happiness, well-being, and safety. Let those come in through the top of your head and flow through your whole body. Keep practicing and I promise, you will be pleasantly surprised!

For those of you who are not familiar with meditation, this is a great place to start your meditation practice. This exercise will begin to allow you to look inside where you will connect to the love, strength, and answers you are seeking that will assist you in helping your special angel find their wings.

Anger as Fuel

After the bus incident, day by day, my anger propelled me onward in my unwavering determination to gain the knowledge I needed to help Chanel get the support she needed to thrive. I knew I had a long road ahead of me, but I was full of confidence that I could do this.

The bus incident happened when Chanel was six years old in the 1st grade and the Camp incident occurred when she was in 6th grade. The bus ride, the camp nightmare, and lots of other incidents regarding Chanel, as well as countless other children I serve, would make this book too long to read if I penned them all. All of these stories have challenged and infuriated me, but as I learned to breathe through the anger, the negative energy transmuted into fuel to make a difference in creating change in the special education system. I had already instinctively known that Chanel was here to teach me and that there was a much bigger picture than I could ever imagine. I had no idea how it would all play out, but I knew that there was a reason and that, more than anything, I needed to practice courage, feel the anger, and keep moving toward my goals.

Every day, I was faced with the choice to move toward love or live in fear and rage. Being a spiritual seeker, this was a huge opportunity for me to practice my faith. Every Sunday at church, I would pray for understanding, strength, and courage. I knew that there was a plan and purpose for all of it, but it was not yet clear to me. Thank heavens my dear friend, Lisa, was always there for me with her listening, supportive ear.

Little did I know that out of the darkness would emerge many rich treasures that were far beyond anything I could have ever dreamed or imagined.

After the bus incident, I continued to grow in my knowledge of how to navigate the broken and unjust system as well as manage my anger. I continued to successfully implement IDEA and acquire the right services for my daughter. Soon, many other parents began asking me to accompany them to their IEP meetings and assist in developing their child's IEP. As I was able to assist them and their angels, I became more passionately motivated to help parents of children with autism and many other disabilities—to empower them to become a knowledgeable and effective IEP team member and to learn to be an advocate for their own child. I quickly became aware of the countless families who were experiencing the injustice and undeniable failure of our system. These unimaginable events in the lives of special needs children had to be addressed, and I was getting ready to do whatever it took to promote and create a system reform.

The Ripe Fig

"Now that You live here in my chest,
anywhere we sit is a mountaintop.
And those other images,
which have enchanted people
like porcelain dolls from China,
which have made men and women
weep for centuries,
even those have changed now.
What used to be pain is a lovely bench
where we can rest under the roses.
A left hand has become a right.
A dark wall, a window.
A cushion in a shoe heel,
the leader of the community!
Now silence. What we say
is poison to some
and nourishing to others.
What we say is a ripe fig,
but not every bird that flies eats figs."

Rumi
The Essential Rumi

CHAPTER 3

TRUMPETS OF JUSTICE

"Chanel's doctor said that she needs Occupational Therapy. Can you help me with this, Mrs. Grace?" I could hardly contain my excitement about this new therapy for Chanel. I just had a feeling that it was going to be a breakthrough for her.

"Occupational Therapy is a therapy given to a child that has a *physical* handicap. Chanel does not have any need for OT, Mrs. Aprahamian." Her voice was monotone, as though she were reading from a script.

I took a deep breath to manage the anger that came up to fight her condescending tone and unwillingness to help me. "The doctor that specializes in autism recommended this for Chanel. She said that the school district provides this for children with autism."

"I don't know what to tell you, Mrs. Aprahamian, but Chanel does not need OT." Now she sounded put-out.

Really? I'm putting YOU out?!?

I instinctively knew that she was misinforming me and that they weren't going to help me obtain the services that Chanel required. Incensed at her flagrant indifference toward my child and me, I did my research and got the answers I needed. Turns out this special education staff member was blatantly lying to me. She knew that kids with autism received OT and that it was a common therapy for children on the spectrum, but she also knew that I was the parent of a newly diagnosed child and that I didn't have the knowledge I needed to defend my request.

I was determined to never allow another school district staff member to get away with trying to cheat my child of what she needed.

In my insatiable desire to learn everything I could about special education, I attended every conference, school district in-service, credited class, and Internet resource I could fit into my schedule. I also became active in many different disability organizations, education groups, and law and advocacy foundations, making connections that educated and supported me in my efforts for years to come.

The Advocate's Work

The amount of information required to be a good advocate is not restricted to just being an expert in special education law and learning the politics of each district's culture. Being a good advocate requires a high level of knowledge in autism as well as a good understanding of all other disabilities. This knowledge is then applied to develop an appropriate Individualized Education Plan, which includes careful crafting of annual goals and objectives that are based upon the student's present levels of academic performance. Identification of the appropriate accommodations and possible need for modifications of academic curriculum is imperative for a student's success. Supports and services include all specialized therapies and remedial and behavioral intervention, which is the heart of the IEP, and a skilled advocate knows which supports and services their client may require.

These supports and services may include Speech and Language Therapy, Occupational Therapy, Applied Behavior Analysis, Physical Therapy, Adaptive Physical Education, Assistive Technology, One on One aide or classroom aide support, Auditory Integration Therapy, Vision Therapy, Counseling, and Remedial Reading Programs. A respected advocate is successful in obtaining the supports and services that each individual child requires in order for the student to receive educational benefit from their special education program.

The provision of supports and services are based on the assessment findings that substantiate the need for that particular service. This initial assessment is conducted in the area of the students suspected disability by an employee of that district. It is common for the district assessment to find the child ineligible for services, so a good advocate knows how to utilize the appeal process. Getting the school district to provide services may require disagreement with the district's assessment and request for an Individual Educational Evaluation (IEE). This is an assessment that is done by a private sector and funded by the school district. This second opinion, which is conducted by a specialist who is not an employee of the school district, is used to provide the evidence needed to find the child eligible for services and requires the school district to fund the service. An experienced advocate can interpret assessment findings, which include standardized test scores, observations, and parent and teacher rating scales. Each service—Speech and Language, Occupational Therapy, ABA, etc.—has it's own language and a knowledgeable advocate understands them all.

Finally, an advocate knows how to take all of this evidence and speak on the child's behalf at IEP meetings to advocate for the supports and services that child requires.

Representation of a student includes writing legally sound letters to document the evidence and parent requests and ensure that the IEP documentation is done correctly. All documentation will trigger specific timelines that require the district to take action to implement the services. A true advocate knows how to use IDEA to hold the district accountable to adhering to these timelines as well as all parent rights to implement the services and the IEP in a timely manner. Lastly, one of the most important skills that an advocate must acquire is the ability to conduct themselves in an ethical, professional, and collaborative manner.

Get Involved

I recommend that parents become active and utilize the unlimited resources available to them both locally and through the Internet, especially in their local CAC (Community Advisory Committee). This is a State mandated committee that consists of parents of special needs children and special education administrators. As a parent, getting involved in your local CAC allows you to build relationships with your local school district special education staff and become knowledgeable about your district's special education department. The CAC meets every month and conducts parent information nights throughout each year to educate and build collaborative relationships between parents and district staff. This will assist you greatly to develop an appropriate IEP for your child.

Time for a Change

In 2004, I went to Sacramento with a group of advocates from my area to attend the reauthorization of IDEA. It was exciting and informative. This experience fueled my motivation to change the way school districts worked with parents. By learning even more about special education law, I could not understand why school districts did not adhere to these laws and why they did not respect parents as a vital member of the IEP team. I was empowered by the new laws and regulations that had been put into place by the 2004 Reauthorization and felt even more passionate about creating a systems reform in my own school district.

When parents hire me to become their advocate, some of the most common questions they immediately ask me are:

- "Why doesn't the school district give my child the services they obviously need?"

- "Why didn't the teacher tell me my child might have a learning disability and that I should ask for special education?"

- "I thought that the school was doing everything that was right and utilizing everything that was available for my child, and I trusted them when they told me to sign my IEP. Now my child is so far behind in their education. They never told me I could ask for additional services or special therapy that could help my child to learn."

- "When I asked for an aide, my principal told me they did not have one available."

- "When I asked the special education teacher what additional help my child could receive in reading, I was told there weren't any services like that."

- "Someone from my school told me that I should hire an advocate but they made me promise I wouldn't mention that they gave me this information. Why aren't educators and service providers allowed to tell parents that they should ask for help or give us any information about getting services for our children?"

School districts are a bureaucracy and therefore work under the rules of a bureaucracy, which means that anyone who is not a district employee is an outsider. Basically, school district administrators supervise the principal who runs the school and supervises the teachers who teach the children, but the district administrators are the gatekeepers of the funding. It is the parent's job to learn this system and know how to utilize their parental rights by building respectful, professional relationships with school district administrators in order to persuade these gatekeepers to provide the services that their child needs.

Every district has it's own climate or culture in which they function in terms of special education. If the special education administrators at the district level are willing to work collaboratively with parents and are inclusive-minded, that district will most likely be functioning well with parents by facilitating successful IEP meetings. When a district's special education administration does not work with parents and discriminates against special education students, that district will most likely have great difficulty with parents who need to employ advocates and attorneys. The same is true at the school site level. The school site administrators and principals who set the tone and model their version of appropriate engagement with parents and students, set the precedence on how to deal with parents.

When a parent hires me and I attend the first IEP meeting in their district, I know immediately what kind of culture that school site functions within. I have developed the ability to read people and I will know if the principal is "special ed friendly" or whether they are indifferent to their special education students and therefore, are most likely violating parental rights.

Enlisting Support

By this time, I had been running a parent support group meeting for three years. This group focused on empowering parents to learn their parental rights under the California Special Education Code. I continued to facilitate this group for another eight years.

During that time, at every parent meeting, the subject of discussion centered on the injustice and contempt of special education staff and their lack of willingness to serve our children. Conversations quickly escalated to parents expressing their outrage and exasperation regarding their child's IEP.

"We need to do something about the way the district is allowing IEP meetings to be run!" demanded a parent.

"They are outright lying to us and refusing to help our kids!" another parent cried out in distress.

"The way they treat us is shameless and spiteful. What can we do, Valerie?"

I knew exactly what we needed to do, and I'd been waiting for the opportunity to get the commitment from the parents to retain Bill Smith to lead the systems reform.

While attending a TASH (a foundation that advocates for inclusion for students on IEP's) special education conference, I had met another strong advocate, who I will call Bill Smith for confidentiality purposes. Bill Smith, a non-attorney advocate, focused his work specifically on holding adversarial school districts accountable under IDEA. School districts did not want Bill to be an active advocate in their district because they knew that he would reveal the violations and problematic culture in their district.

In the mid 90's, it was common for most districts to work with parents in an unethical manner by giving misinformation, violating timelines by delaying provision of services, and blatantly coercing, intimidating, and retaliating against parents in IEP meetings. There were many stories of how school site staff retaliated against the student of the parents who were advocating within our group. This is a huge violation of IDEA and should not be tolerated in any form. Parents should never be afraid to advocate for their child at the risk of having their child discriminated against during the school day. Bill also had a child with the diagnosis of autism, and our similar mission to create a system change had a powerful impact in the development of my advocacy journey.

Here it goes! I thought, as I felt my heart expand and my whole body awakened with anticipation. *It's time. Let's do it!*

"We need to join together and organize a plan to change the way our district fails to provide special education for our children. We can do this if we work together. There is power in numbers! It isn't going to be easy and we are going to encounter an enormous amount of turbulence and resistance. It is going to take commitment, both emotionally and financially."

"We don't care, Valerie. We want change and we want our kids to get the services they need. We are done playing these games and being treated like this!"

That was all I needed to hear to begin working my plan. I began pursuing Bill Smith to ask him to assist my parent group to lead a system reform in my school district. Bill was a very busy advocate and he also lived quite a distance away from my area. He explained that when he takes on this kind of a case, it takes at least a year or more of constant work and commitment to do this kind of a job. He outlined the financial requirements and time commitment he needed from the group to allow him to make the decision to lead the reform. His requirements included a commitment from me to assist him every step of the way. Of course, I anxiously agreed. Soon, Bill had *moved* to my hometown so he would be accessible and available to work intensively on this endeavor.

Because I had been so active in the special needs community through advocating for children and teaching special education law classes, I had established a large number of relationships with parents of special needs children in my area. I quickly gathered thirty-five families together to join the reform group. These parents were extremely angry about their child's lack of progress and services. Each of them had their own story to tell about the lies, disrespect, and adversarial manner in which the school staff and IEP team had treated these parents and failed to meet the needs of their child. Fourteen parents filed for Due Process. Three of those fourteen cases actually went to hearing. The others were resolved in Mediation or dispute resolution sessions. We filed compliance complaints with the State Board of Education. We attended school board meetings with large groups of parents and presented our stories to the school board. Several articles were written in our local newspaper regarding the special education hearings and the large amount of parents who were attending school board meetings.

Due Process Hearing

A Due Process Hearing is the formal, legal procedure that resolves differences about special education services for your student with the goal to ensure a free and appropriate public education (FAPE) tailored to your student's unique needs. Disputes can arise concerning eligibility, placement, services, and/or supports for your student. Both the parent and the school district have the right to file for a Due Process Hearing to resolve a dispute. In 2005, the U.S. Supreme Court decided (Schaffer v. Weast) that the party who files the Due Process Complaint has the burden of proving whether the child's rights are being protected or whether the individualized educational program (IEP) is appropriate.

Resistance and Intimidation

"Your client refused to comply with district policy!" screamed the attorney. "You need to get your client under control, Mrs. Aprahamian!" Vengeance dripped from her tone.

"Stop yelling at her!" my client screamed back at the attorney, trying to protect me from the lawyer's ugly attack.

I patted my client's leg, reassuring her that I was fine and that I could handle the aggressive assault of the district's counsel.

The school site principal and district coordinator silently observed from across the table of the conference room at the IEP meeting with despicable grins on their faces.

Bill taught me to not be intimidated by school district administrators. I was well-educated in special education law and knew the game of power and manipulation that districts play when they become adversarial. I knew that it was the district who had violated IDEA regulations and that the parent had every right to disagree with their offer of FAPE. Therefore, I did not need to yell or even respond to the unprofessional manner of the district counsel. I'm sure she thought that because I was not a lawyer, she could intimidate me by yelling and threatening me or scare me enough to back down on my mission of reform. My lack of reaction only made her more incensed.

This warlike confrontation continued for another hour as the district counsel tried to thwart my challenge of the district's precedence to violate parental rights. I continued to experience many IEP meetings just like this one as we continued to pursue our reform movement, but I wouldn't let them stop me.

They just could not believe that our group of parents dared to defy them by standing on our parental rights and demanding that our children be served. It was typical protocol for special education staff to have their own agenda and predetermine each student's placement and services, which completely omitted a parent's input as an IEP team member. Predetermining the outcome of a child's IEP is a violation of IDEA.

I continued to work, night and day, completely immersed in my mission to make a positive change for the children. Because of the time, energy, and mental focus this endeavor required, I could not fulfill my typical role as a mother on my own. My husband had to fill in the gaps for me in caring for my children. I missed out on many dinners with the family and time spent with my children and husband because we were in the middle of a hearing or preparing for an IEP meeting. I even missed out on attending many Sunday morning church services as a family because Bill and I were always under a timeline to get things completed. Yet, I somehow managed to continue my FETA parent support group meetings at the church. My kids were in intermediate school and it was not easy for any of us, but my husband and my children knew the importance of what I was doing and they supported me because they loved Chanel and they loved all the other special needs children that were going to benefit from the reform. It took great sacrifice, but what we accomplished was worth it all.

One weekend, Bill decided that we needed some fun time with our families, so we took a few days off and went to an amusement park. All the kids had a blast going on the roller coasters and just being together. They still remember that day as a family because I was absent so much of that year.

When Bill and I would be working in my office in my home, Chanel would come in and give Bill a big hug. And if Jessica was home, she too, would join in with a group hug. My kids loved Bill because they knew what he was doing for them and all the kids who needed services, so they could have a positive future.

Tools for Advocacy: Compliance Complaints

A Compliance Complaint is a specific kind of complaint written to the California Board of Education in Sacramento. This is a very powerful tool in advocacy because the State Board of Education will investigate the parent's complaint to determine whether or not the parent's allegations are factual and whether or not the California Education Code was truly violated. If the results of the investigation find the school district in violation of the California Education Code, the results become public record. If a district is found to have excessive violations within one school year, the state may decide to withhold special education funding from that district.

A Compliance Complaint is therefore a tool for advocates to hold districts accountable to adhere to the California Education Code, which is mandated under IDEA, which is federal law. These laws provide parent rights as well as hold districts accountable to timelines for provisions of special education supports and services in the development of a child's Individual Education Program (IEP).

Every two weeks, the local school district will conduct a school board meeting. This is also a very powerful way to address your concerns regarding your child's IEP because parents are given the opportunity to present their concerns and complaints by telling their story to the local school district board and school district officials who attend school board meetings. The meetings are televised locally and are also public record. Each parent is given approximately three minutes to present his or her concern to the board, so it's important to be well-prepared.

School district administrators spend most of their time in the office attending meetings with other school district officials, so they are not out at school sites, nor are they typically exposed to what is actually happening on school campuses. Unless your case goes to hearing, school board officials rarely know what is actually going on regarding specific special education cases. This is why speaking before the board is a powerful way to bring your case information to high-level district administrators.

My favorite resource for parents is Wrightslaw.com. This is a website and free newsletter that will teach you everything you need to know about how to become an excellent advocate for your special needs child. There are many books available for sale on this website, written by Pete Wright, a prominent Special Education attorney who works on behalf of parents and their child. Pete Wright travels the nation, offering Special Education

Law workshops for parents. I highly recommend all parents experience one of Pete's conferences in an effort to empower yourself with the knowledge you require to meet the needs of your child.

I recently attended the Special Education Law Institute Attorney and non-Attorney Advocate credentialed program, located at the William and Mary University in Virginia. This program is part of Pete Wright's endeavor to teach Special Education Law to lawyers and non-attorney advocates.

I worked tirelessly with Bill for over a year representing parents in countless IEP meetings and many hearings. Bill and I organized the groups that presented at the school board meetings and would open the session with our speech on behalf of the group. Within the group that Bill and I gathered, many couples came together. Consequently, the husband and the wife both presented their story about their child. Some meetings would last up to three hours because we had so many families attending to speak before the board and convey their stories about their individual special education student. This kind of thing was unprecedented. It was unusual at school board meetings to have even a few people speak during open forum. During most typical meetings, there are no parents there at all. We would regularly hold parent meetings in my home to rally our efforts and plan our next steps.

Success!

And then, on one glorious and magnificent day our efforts were rewarded! The district decided that they needed to make a change and begin to work collaboratively with parents and honor parental rights in meeting the needs of special education students. A little over a year after we began our parent movement, new staff members that were willing to work collaboratively with parents had replaced the SELPA Director, Special Education Director, and many of the Program Specialists who had been at the helm of the previously adversarial administration.

They look like they are trying to listen to us. Let's see if they chose people who actually care about parents and students more than their own bureaucracies and egos.

As I walked into the Special Education department, my stomach fluttered with anticipation. The new SELPA Director had scheduled a meeting with me at her office to get acquainted. I was pleasantly surprised at this invitation, yet I remained cautious about her intention.

"Mrs. Aprahamian, it is a pleasure to meet you. My intention is for us to work together for the benefit of the children, and I am responsible for working with the special education staff in an effort to transform the way in which we work with parents and with you. I do not want any further adversarial feelings between us and the parents of these children who need services. We are going to learn how to collaborate as a team during IEP meetings in an effort to work toward serving the children."

I could not believe what I was hearing!

Am I dreaming? Could she really be sincere? Will she really stay committed and be successful in creating a change in leadership at the district level?

"This is all I have ever wanted and has always been my intention as an advocate," I replied in full agreement. "I never wanted to fight or be adversarial, but we didn't have a choice. We had to take action for the sake of our children. I hope you understand that. I *fully* support you in this endeavor and give you my word that I will do everything I can to build collaborative and trusting relationships between parents and special education staff members."

I wanted to get up and do a happy dance in the middle of the school district office as we continued to talk about the turbulent relationships between parents and district staff and brainstorm strategies to begin building trust and collaboration.

I left her office excited and encouraged with the outcome of our conversation, but still a little apprehensive.

Is this really possible? Is it the beginning of a new era for special education in this school district? Has the vision that I have dreamed about for so many years actually blossomed into a real possibility?

It was a positive and miraculous shift in the lives of many families of special needs children as well as in the life and education of my own daughter, Chanel. I hold the highest regard for this administrator, who was responsible for spearheading a fundamental change in the district's culture in terms of how they perceived and interacted with parents in special education. My local school district is now known as a school district that meets the needs of all children and aspires to work collaboratively with parents. Their reputation is so positive that parents actually move within the district's boundaries in order to work with these district administrators. I truly believe this is possible for every district, if the parents take responsibility for knowing and defending their rights.

Systemic Change and Collaboration

Because this shift in administration held the conviction to include parents as viable IEP team members, my business model changed drastically and my role was redefined as an advocate. Instead of fighting for the parents and children, my task was to build collaborative working relationships with district staff members. The "us against them" precedence that had been set for so many years was now a thing of the past, and so I approached each meeting as a team player and encouraged parents and the other IEP team members to do the same.

This shift in my advocacy career was perfectly aligned with my transition in moving out of anger and opened me up to moving though the rest of the grief process.

As a mother, my emotions were painful and overwhelming. As an advocate, it was difficult for me to forget the countless special angels that the district failed to serve, year after year. These feelings of anger and frustration toward the school district only made it more difficult to come to an agreement during IEP meetings. Honestly, it made it incredibly hard for me to stay calm during a meeting as we moved through the transition to a new way of working together as a team. There were many times when the IEP meetings would revert back to old patterns, which challenged me to learn how to look at district staff as people instead of the enemy.

It is difficult to let go of the anger that we feel as a result of the horrific experiences that we have endured. How could we not feel angry and incensed with stories like Chanel's bus ride, camping experience, and the fight to have her educated in an inclusion model year after year? We are faced with trying to work with the injustice of a bureaucratically-based system in which administrators believe they somehow have the right to interpret the California Education Code according to their own agenda at the cost of our children's education, health, and safety.

This has been a great lesson for me in my journey in learning how to recognize opportunities to grow in difficult situations. I let go of the belief that I need to fight out of anger and moved to a place of building a collaborative support team with a unified purpose.

Now in order to look at things objectively, it is important to look at both sides of every story. I want to clarify that I am not making a global statement that all special education staff members are insincere in their intention to work with parents. There are many who have made education their career because they love teaching and want to make a difference in the lives of children. I am simply presenting the whole picture of the truth about the reality of parents and educators trying to work within an educational system that is based upon a bureaucracy.

The point I am making is that we must remember that we are working with people who are required to work within the constraints of district policies. If we can approach the IEP team members as people with feelings and emotions just like ours, we will be more successful in building relationships that will enable us to work together.

Because of the success we achieved as a result of the reform, I let go of my anger and changed my perspective. I found that most educators truly believe in their hearts that they are doing the right thing and that they are following the policies and procedures mandated for their job. It was a huge shift in my perception, but I suddenly realized that they are people too, and most of them are doing the best they can do with what they have. This shift in my perspective changed the tone of all of my IEP meetings, and it quickly shifted the trajectory of my clients' children's education.

Recently, a couple hired me to speak on their behalf. The father kept repeating over and over, "They are just not good people. They are just bad people. Why are they doing this to our family?" It is easy to come to this conclusion when we live through experiences that are simply terrifying and unjust under the supervision and facilitation of school district staff members. But, if we can keep an open mind and realize that we are working with people and not just "school district staff members," maybe we can change our perspective a bit.

Since the successful reform, I have built many wonderful, trusting relationships with school site staff and district administrators. After working together in hundreds of successful IEP meetings, I am welcomed and respected as a non-adversarial advocate to the district. Many of them know that I am not the enemy and that my intention as an advocate is to work in good faith with district staff. The majority of them believe that my role is to speak on behalf of the family with the intention of building a unified IEP team with the goal of meeting the needs of the child. It is a wonderful place to be as an advocate and allows me to be extremely successful because of the valued reputation I have been able to build over the years since the reform.

When we learn our parental rights and begin to implement them without all of the anger driving it, we can begin to drive our children's education and actually make a difference in our local school district.

Do It for Your Angel

Here is another opportunity for you to journal. Write about those situations that you have experienced that are similar to my stories about IEP nightmares, problematic teachers, and education challenges. Look at your anger and feelings of betrayal that you may feel toward school site staff and administrators. Write about how you felt in that situation and try and process your emotions. Did you feel misled or deceived? Was your trust violated?

Do you feel that the system betrayed you and your child?

Do you blame yourself for not knowing any better and feel you should have taken action sooner? If this is you, please realize that every parent comes to this realization at a certain point, and that is usually when they decide to get help and end up in my office. What I tell parents is that feeling guilty is not going to serve you or your child, but leaving the past behind while setting the intention to move forward by working to develop the most appropriate IEP is the ultimate goal of every parent.

Now ask yourself: Have I educated myself to know how to implement my parental rights? If I were to be in this situation again, how could I use IDEA to address this situation?

The best advocacy tip I can give you is to empower yourself with the knowledge to implement your role as a vital member of the IEP team. Did you know that you are an equal IEP team member and have equal power in comparison to any other member of the IEP team? Under IDEA, you have more power than you could ever imagine, so please step into that power by educating yourself on the IEP process and take a leadership role at your next IEP meeting. It will be the best thing you could ever do for your child's education.

Have you become an expert in the area of your child's disability and how it relates to your parental rights in the development of your child's IEP? When you have had a disagreement at an IEP, have you documented your concerns in a letter? Did you ensure that your concerns were documented in your IEP? Have you begun to learn about what a measurable and specific goal and objective should look like? Have you begun to read your child's assessments and learn how to interpret the standardized test scores? Have you utilized the opportunity to file a compliance complaint or attended a school board meeting? If in fact you have implemented your parental rights, can you let go of your anger and move forward by establishing and developing respectful working relationships with your IEP team?

A special needs child's education will determine their future and whether or not they will be able to become an independent community member who can successfully hold a job. Without early intervention and appropriate therapies and services, these students will end up living with their parents for most of their lives and then most likely end up being placed in a group home for adults with disabilities. In these homes, many of the individuals are abused and discriminated against. The majority of these homes are not a place where any parent would want their loved one to be.

At your next IEP meeting, place a picture of your child on the table and bring the team's intention to working toward the ultimate outcome of the meeting, which is your child's education and future. This is a great way to visually keep your child as the focus of your IEP meeting and will neutralize the personalities, opinions, power plays and funding concerns that may jeopardize the principals of the IEP meeting.

When advocates, parents, and school district staff learn how to work together as a team in the best interest of the child in order to meet their educational needs according to Special Education Code, we are all successful. We can work together with our local school district to help these most extraordinary individuals that have been placed within our responsibility and tender loving care. If we can focus our efforts on the ultimate goal of aspiring to adhere to the principals of IDEA, we can make great strides in working together in the best interest of all children with an IEP.

Parents along with our local school districts have been awarded the profound privilege and ultimate obligation to pave the way for these special angels by meeting their educational needs to reach the highest expression of themselves in their lives here on earth.

It was a great victory, and the elation was palpable in our district as the changes began to occur. I cheered with every change, not realizing that there was even more change on the horizon for me…change that would cause the collapse of my very foundation and challenge me to dig deep to get to the other side.

"Listen to your heart, it harbors sacred things.
Give from your heart; abundance it brings.
Pray through your heart; guidance in need.
Follow your heart, it knows how to lead."

Paul Mark Sutherland

CHAPTER 4

TEAR DROPS FROM HEAVEN

As I stood in my backyard, watching a pool full of special needs kids joyfully swimming, I was profoundly aware of the power of community. It was so nice to see all the parents casually talking amongst themselves, as we enjoyed the beautiful summer day together.

It warmed my heart to see Chanel approach Jimmy to welcome him to the pool party. Jimmy was Bill's son, who also had the diagnosis of autism. Jimmy was anxiously running back and forth from the pool through the gate toward his car and back again. Feeling overwhelmed with the large amount of kids and parents, he was having a hard time settling in to enjoy the party. Chanel calmly took Jimmy's hand and tried to lead him toward the pool. Even though Jimmy and Chanel were non-verbal at that time, they seemed to communicate in their own secret way.

It was the annual swim party I hosted for all the families, clients, and friends who had children with special needs. I employed Junior Life Guards for the pool party to keep the kids safe while they swam, which allowed parents a much-deserved respite with fellow parents. This year, the party was exceptionally large as it was the year of the movement to change our local school district. This group had a solidified connection because we shared in the excitement of such an amazing and powerful victory, not only for our children but also for the future children who would receive special education within our local school district.

"Valerie, we have a special gift for you." One of the parents handed me a beautiful box, wrapped in gold shiny paper. All the parents gathered around, with cunning smiles on their faces, anticipating my reaction to the surprise they had so covertly planned for me.

"What is this?" I asked with unexpected delight.

"Just open it and you'll see!" Their excitement increased mine.

I unveiled a beautiful plaque made of glass with an etched message held between two roman columns. The message read: *With much appreciation, we honor Valerie Aprahamian, for all your hard work and heartfelt efforts in assuring our children's success. Thank you. Love, The Families You Have Blessed*

My heart was filled with gratitude and awe that I was a part of this amazing experience. This plaque meant so much because it was like an altar of remembrance for this transitional period in my life and in the lives of so many families within our special needs community.

Although our efforts were successful in creating a positive systems change in the special education department in our local school district, the victory required an enormous amount of hard work, sacrifice, perseverance, and many life lessons…some of which were incredibly painful.

The Beginning of the End

"Hello, Valerie, this is Mrs. Denise Brown (whose name has been changed for confidentiality). I need to speak to you about the FETA (From Emotions To Advocacy) class you teach for the parents. I'm sorry, but you are not going to be able to facilitate your meetings at the church any longer because the content and purpose of your meetings is not biblically based," she explained coldly.

My heart dropped and that anger started to bubble to the surface, but I tried to contain it. "Really, Denise? I've been holding this support group for over two years and now you suddenly have decided that it isn't biblically based? You originally loved the idea of having my special needs parent group be a part of your disabilities ministry!"

"I am sorry, but you will only be allowed to have the meeting in which the SELPA Director is speaking, the one that has already been planned, but that will be your last meeting here at the church." Her voice was flat, except for a tinge of irritation before she said goodbye and hung up.

The new SELPA Director at my local school district had agreed to conduct a special presentation at an upcoming FETA meeting at the church. Essentially, it was a peace offering in the process of developing a collaborative relationship to work together for the benefit of families. It was very unusual for a District Special Education Administrator to do something like this because it was outside the realm of her job requirements, and it meant a great deal to me. I held the utmost respect for her because she was going out of her way to show her support of my work, which was to empower families in our local school district.

At least they're letting me hold that meeting, I thought as I slammed the phone down on the counter.

More than 100 people attended and the meeting was a huge success.

Yet they still refused to allow me to continue my meetings at their location.

This just doesn't make sense that they would stop my parent meetings after such a successful event. I had 100 parents show up! To have this kind of turnout for a special needs event is very rare. I am quite sure Mrs. Brown's disability ministry events were not as successful. Don't they see this as a benefit for the church disability ministry?

Since Mrs. Brown's telephone call, I just couldn't shake the suspicious irritation in my stomach.

I can't help but believe that Mrs. Brown is doing this because of what happened with Joey? Even though she's a special education teacher, she doesn't want to teach a student with autism who has maladaptive behaviors she doesn't want to deal with…she would rather throw him in a Severely Handicapped Class, where he would only focus on functional skills, not an academic curriculum…and I called her on it in an IEP meeting…and now she's doing this…what are the chances? This is more than just a coincidence.

I knew this all came down to an inclusion issue and a LRE situation. Joey had the right to remain in a non-severely handicapped class, and Mrs. Brown wanted to segregate him in the most restrictive placement.

The dots started to connect, but I didn't want to believe it. This is not how a beloved Christian sister would act… or would she?

*Isn't teaching parents how to advocate for their special needs child's education, so they can live a more successful life, a Christian thing to do? Isn't **that** supporting and loving families within our community? Doesn't this support group* *provide community outreach to bring in new families to attend this church?*

Even though I experienced this discouraging situation with the church for the third time (yes, I'd tried to support special needs families at two previous locations, only to have politics and other people's discomfort with special needs children's differences get in the way of the ministry's success), I continued to have faith that I could still be involved with a special needs ministry by teaching parents special education law.

Inclusion applies to all communities. Any community, organization, educational program, and society in general, will not grow or be successful if division is tolerated and unity and inclusion is not practiced.

Why can't they see that by allowing this separation, they are creating division and polarity within the Church? I looked up from the phone and saw Chanel compliantly working with her after-school academic tutor. Her tutor's daughter frequently came with her mom to interact with Chanel and help her with her social skills and, when I looked up from my upsetting phone call, Chanel was laughing with Sara as they worked on a project together. *See! She wouldn't have been able to be that compliant and appropriately socialize with a peer so well if she had been segregated and not treated as an equally valuable human being. Why can't they see that these special angels reflect unconditional love when we put them in the right environments and give them the support they need?*

Attempting Inclusion in Church

I grew up attending a Presbyterian church every Sunday and the Christian religion was my spiritual foundation. As an adult, I attended a non-denominational church, and became heavily involved with the Christian community, which served as a large part of my life and my identity.

As a child, I felt as if I was born with an internal knowing of my connection to God and had a strong desire to grow in my knowledge and understanding of the Bible and spirituality. As a young adult, in my quest to know God, I attended a college of theology. Simply put, I have always been a spiritual seeker.

After Michael and I were married, we attended church every Sunday and raised our kids going to Sunday school. I was on the Women's Ministry Board and volunteered countless hours to this ministry. My closest friendships developed from going to church, and I couldn't have imagined my life any other way.

But after Chanel was born, I found myself dismayed with the church because of the void in ministry to special needs children and their families. I wanted to encourage the church to learn how to better assist parents of children diagnosed with autism. In an effort to make a difference, I became involved with MOPS (Mothers of Preschoolers) as a board member. I was a regular on the MOPS speaking circuit and traveled all over Orange County to provide information about inclusive disabilities ministries and encourage the MOPS board members throughout Southern California to develop this model for their organization.

In addition to holding a seat on the board of the Women's Ministry and MOPS, along with my speaking engagements, I began my parent support group, FETA (From Emotions to Advocacy) where I taught Special Education Law.

The church is a place where families come for support and understanding in their time of need. Why isn't the church acknowledging all of these families that are in crisis because parents are having children diagnosed with autism? Why are congregation members turning a blind eye to the fact that these families (my own family included) need love and support? Isn't the whole point of Christianity to love one another unconditionally?

At this time, in the early 1990's, there were just a handful of churches that had disabilities ministries and all of them provided segregated Sunday school classes for special needs children. So essentially, parents were faced with segregation, discrimination, and polarity not only at school but also at their church …in a place where love was supposed to reign.

The bible says, *"As Jesus passed by, he saw a man blind from birth. And his disciples asked him, 'Rabbi, who sinned, this man or his parents, that he was born blind?' Jesus answered, 'It was not that this man sinned, or his parents, but that the works of God might be displayed in him."* (John 9:1-3)

Why does the church, as a whole, insist on having a special place for them to go…why can't they just be with all the rest of the kids? I felt a passionate calling and deep responsibility to address the fact that the church was excluding families and segregating special needs children by not including these special angels as part of the typical congregation.

The church I was attending did not have a special needs ministry at all. I was successfully holding the parent support group, but the pastoral staff had little interest in going any further regarding the special needs ministry. We only had two special needs kids there, and one was my daughter Chanel. Chanel didn't cause any issues in Sunday school and neither did the other little boy with Downs Syndrome.

After many years of trying to develop a disabilities ministry within my church, I finally realized that I needed to move on to work with a pastor who supported my desire to develop an inclusive disabilities ministry. This was not an easy decision because our family had many close friends that attended our congregation and we had created years of wonderful memories with my kids growing up in this church. In spite of my sentiment and because of my desire to live my purpose, I could not excuse the fact that the support I needed from the pastoral staff to create a special needs ministry *just wasn't there.*

I learned about a church nearby who had a pastor I felt would be open to my calling, I wrote a letter of appeal and described my burning desire to raise awareness about autism and the lack of ministry to Christian families dealing with a child with a disability. He was open and willing to strongly support me to develop an "inclusive special needs ministry" within his church. In fact, this pastor was very passionate about my vision and had been looking for someone to fill this role in his church!

So I relocated my parent support group to my new church home and developed a ministry for children with disabilities to attend typical Sunday school with an aide. At that time, there were close to 6,000 students on IEP's in our district. My vision was to encourage parents from our district area to begin attending my new church because we would be able to offer them an inclusive Sunday school. Coupled with meeting the needs of the countless Christian families who lacked a church home because their autistic child was not welcomed in Sunday school, this was an opportunity to raise awareness within the Christian community and create unity within the church. I had a big dream and I was overflowing with passion and enthusiasm to make it a reality.

I decided to utilize the youth group as a way to develop potential aides. This would give teens the opportunity to have the enriching experience of working with a child with a disability as well as provide aide staffing for the ministry. I facilitated trainings for the Youth Group and children's ministry staff to train the teens how to assist a peer or younger child with special needs in the typical Sunday school class. In this training, I focused on providing knowledge and education regarding what autism was and why these kids display stereotypical behaviors.

The lessons in unconditional love began during those trainings.

One of my favorite and most effective exercises to facilitate was an interactive lesson in which a student could actually experience what it is like for a child on the spectrum to be in a classroom. A volunteer would play an autistic student and sit on the stage at a desk in a chair. I had a very, very bright light shining directly in their eyes and two other kids on either side of them talking to each other in a conversation. Another student rolled the student's chair around and around, while yet another student had scratch paper and would lightly be irritating the student's skin. In the background, a sound machine played a "buzzing" noise. All this would be happening while I was the "teacher" at the front of the class, instructing him on a lesson he was expected to learn.

The student who volunteered was astonished to find how difficult it was to try and learn in spite of the sensory distractions that impeded his focus and attention, and my point was easy to make: "This is just a snapshot for us in understanding what it is like for a child with the diagnosis of sensory integration disorder and what they experience in the classroom. This is the reason why autistic kids may spin, flap their hands, stomp their feet, or rock in their chair and make sounds. They are trying to modulate their sensory system."

After experiencing this powerful exercise, the youth could easily understand the challenges that these kids face on a daily basis. Their eyes were opened to feel compassion and understanding, which gave them the buy-in they needed to promote and support this ministry.

Sensory Integration Dysfunction/ Sensory Processing Disorder

Many children on the autism spectrum also have sensory deficits. Sensory processing disorder can significantly affect a child's ability to learn and be successful in completing typical everyday tasks. Many parents don't understand and are not even aware that their child has sensory issues and needs occupational therapy.

Sensory integration dysfunction (SID) or sensory processing disorder (SPD) is a term that refers to the way the nervous system receives messages from the five senses—sight, touch, sound, taste, smell, and movement—and turns them into appropriate motor and behavioral responses. Everything we do is modulated by our sensory integration whether it is eating, physical activity, reading and learning, or traveling in a car. It all requires processing sensation or "sensory integration." SID can appear as motor skills clumsiness, behavioral problems, anxiety, depression, and serious school problems, and can affect how one successfully navigates countless everyday tasks.

Sensory Processing Disorder can look very different from one student to the next. One child may over-respond to sensation and be "hyper" sensitive to clothing, physical contact, light, sound, and food, which causes sensory input to be even painful and unbearable, while another student may under-respond or be "hypo" or slow to stimulation which would cause them to seek out stimulation. These kids have a high tolerance of pain or extreme hot and cold, and their posture and motor skills can be affected. These are the "floppy babies" and the kids who get called "klutz" and "spaz" on the playground. Still other children exhibit an appetite for sensation that is in perpetual overdrive. These kids often are misdiagnosed and inappropriately medicated for ADHD.

These difficulties put children with sensory dysfunction at high risk for many emotional, social, and educational problems, including the inability to make friends or be a part of a group, poor self-esteem, academic failure, and being labeled clumsy, uncooperative, belligerent, disruptive, or "out of control." Anxiety, depression, aggression, or other behavior problems can be the result of sensory deficits. Parents may be blamed for their children's behavior if the child is not diagnosed to identify sensory deficits.

Because most parents have never heard of sensory processing disorder, they don't ask their school district for an Occupational Therapy Assessment. An OT assessment would identify a child's sensory deficits and hopefully provide the accommodations, supports, and services needed to address how sensory integration disorder impedes the child's ability to learn in the classroom.

The problem is that OT is one of the most difficult therapies to obtain with most school districts. It is common to hear occupational therapist's quote their scripted jargon to deny services: "Educationally based OT is a collaborative model and is provided within the classroom. It is not a 'clinical' model in which the student is pulled out of the classroom to a sensory room with equipment and one on one direct services with an OT." Many OT's have no knowledge or ability to identify and assess sensory integration; therefore, they only assess fine motor skills. The majority of OT assessment findings will ultimately recommend OT for a fine motor deficit and assist the student with their handwriting only.

In a "collaborative model," the OT meets with the teacher (who is not an OT and may know nothing about SID) and instructs the teacher to give the student a squishy ball or a padded seat cushion or a "break card" so the student may take a break if they look anxious or unable to concentrate. Sadly, this type of OT falls significantly short in meeting the majority of children's sensory needs. Parents should request that a qualified Occupational Therapist, who has a credential in sensory integration (SIPT certified), to provide a program that includes measurable goals and provides equipment in a sensory room in addition to collaboration with the teacher in the classroom.

The disabilities ministry was growing and aides were successfully including kids in Sunday school classes. Because of my vision to take this message to the congregation, I created events and organized fundraisers and received generous gifts for my ministry. I built the special needs ministry fund to a balance of more than $11,000.

It's working! I am so happy! The aides are doing great and the kids are so happy to just go to Sunday school and be like a typical kid. Parents cannot believe that they are actually going to church as a family and their child doesn't have to go to the "special class" with only kids with disabilities.

The pastor and his wife were very supportive of my vision of inclusion within the church and were the key players in assisting me to develop this ministry, but the pastor had become ill about the same time I joined his community. As the pastor's illness worsened, he became less involved in church decisions. Because of his illness, the support for the vision that we shared was increasingly diminishing, and when his illness required him to step down from his position as lead pastor of the church, my ability to continue to build upon my mission to create an "inclusive ministry" was seriously impacted.

After the pastor stepped down from his position, my ideas to facilitate special events were denied repeatedly by the Church Board. I wanted to utilize the special needs ministry funds that I had generated to continue to expand the program and presented plans to hold a conference, hoping they would begin to embed this message into Sunday morning sermons. But I was denied.

I began collaborating with other ministries within the church and continued to have difficulty with the Children's Ministry Director who discouraged me from inclusion and offended parents of children with autism who were a part of my ministry.

In our local school district, there are more than 6,000 students on IEP's. There is a massive population that could be reached and take part in the program right in our own backyard. It would also be an incredible outreach opportunity for the church. What a win/win situation!

Again and again, I was denied approval to utilize the funding I had generated in the disabilities ministry fund. My heart was dismayed with the lack of empathy and unwillingness of the church board to support a ministry that was growing and reaching families within our community.

How can my own church not want inclusion for children with disabilities? How can they turn their backs on so many families who are in crisis and need a church home for their children to attend Sunday school? These parents are struggling and their crisis affects their marriage and relationships and their finances, which affects them emotionally and spiritually. They are faced with hard questions: Where is God in all of this? Why would God allow this to happen to our child and our family? Why isn't there more support and help for us from our own church home? Why aren't we included in the one place that should be the safest and most loving support system?

My heart broke for the parents who would tell me that they couldn't attend their church because their child with autism was not allowed to attend Sunday school. Many parents came up with creative ways to keep attending church. Some couples would not attend church together, and they would take turns, each going to church separately. One parent would go to a service while the other parent would stay home with their autistic child. This is extremely sad in light of the fact that attending church as a couple plays a large role, in many marriages, in strengthening a cohesive spiritual relationship.

I knew that I could not continue my efforts at this church because the hypocrisy I was experiencing was at odds with my core beliefs of Christianity. I longed for a spiritual foundation that taught non-judgment, unconditional love, and inclusion. I could no longer tolerate the restrictive rules and dogma that was based on fear and polarized the equality of all human beings. Although I was definitely discouraged with organized religion, I still had a passion to create a community of parents, as a unified body, to group together to support one another in unconditional love.

I contacted another local church and asked if they would be interested in allowing me to use their facility to conduct my parent support group meetings. This church was a very large church in my city and they already had an established disabilities ministry there but this ministry was a *segregated program*. Since this church was not interested in inclusion, I had no intention of being involved in the disabilities ministry and I would focus my efforts solely on leading the parent support group. I had come to grips with the fact that I had to let go of my interest in developing an inclusive ministry within any church. After hitting a brick wall at two churches while trying to manifest my dream of an inclusive ministry, I decided that I was just ahead of my time as a thought leader. The church was just not ready for this kind of progressive thinking, but I have no doubt that some day, this will be a typical component of many churches across the country.

And so, once again, I moved to another church community. Over the two years that my parent group met at this church, the meetings continued to grow in attendance and reach many families in my community who began to attend the church as a result.

Mrs. Brown was not only the Disabilities Director at this new church location but she also was a Special Education Teacher in my local school district. And I thought, for that reason, that she would be my biggest supporter. (Sigh.)

After Mrs. Brown discontinued my parent support group meeting, I continued to attend this church until about six months later, when I realized that I needed to take a break from attending church. The church community had been my lifelong support system, and letting go of this foundation was extremely difficult for me. Nevertheless, I knew that this decision was the next step I needed to take on my own spiritual path.

Whether that path involves being a churchgoer or creating an individual spiritual practice, the most loving thing we can do is give permission to one another, without judgment, to make that decision. And, I believe that no matter what path one chooses, we are always exactly where we need to be.

After years of pursuing my ideal of raising awareness of special needs families within the church, I came to the realization that I needed to reevaluate this calling. In time, I realized that I was being called away from my mission within the church, which would then give a singular focus of my energy to create change in the educational system. I have learned that there are times that we are "called to" and times we can be "called away." This awareness gave me the permission I needed to begin to let go of religious ritual, which allowed me to begin to create my own personal spiritual practice.

I now realize that this was my opportunity to expand the way I would help families of special needs children in expressing unconditional love as well as begin to explore other avenues of spiritual growth.

I walked through the open door of possibilities as a spiritual seeker and as an advocate.

Angel Love

Our children are here to teach us how to love. Because of their unique ways of relating, communicating, and behaving, they are challenging the way we think and what we value to be true…our definition of love.

Will we continue to segregate autistic children or will we become inclusive minded and love and accept them exactly as they are?

Our Constitution says, "All men are created equally with the freedom to pursue life, liberty, and the pursuit of happiness." And IDEA states that it is every student's civil right to be included in the general educated classroom. There is very specific criterion, which must be followed before removing a student from the general education environment. Best practices show that all students do better in an inclusive educational model.

I believe that's because including them demonstrates more love than placing them in segregated classrooms despite the ridiculous statements of educational staff who state that placing special needs students in typical classrooms causes them to stand out as "different." The truth of the matter is that inclusion often elicits fear in many parents of typical children as well as educators who are unwilling to expand their belief system and learn new ways of teaching.

Whether our foundational ethics are based upon religion, spirituality, science, or just being a good person, when faced with challenges that may jeopardize our belief system, we have a choice to move toward fear or love, segregation or inclusion, separation or oneness.

What is important is that you find the answers that are right for you regarding the questions that have arisen in your own life because of your special needs child.

Do It For Your Angel

Here is another opportunity for you to journal. Write down the questions that have tested your fundamental belief system and answer the following: What have you learned since your child was born? Have you considered the possibility of changing the way in which you view how you think about your child from a "this is so wrong" perspective to the understanding that it can be a gift and an opportunity to learn unconditional love? What in your life has been removed or has fallen apart since your child was born? Do you see the benefit in these things no longer being present in your life by seeing how they no longer serve you in moving forward? Have you considered that your child has given you the opportunity to expand your belief system to a more inclusive way of thinking without judgment?

Continue to make notes as you progress in the process of thinking through these questions. You may not have ever asked yourself some of these questions or you may have never even acknowledged that these issues may be present in your life. If you have already been on a journey of questioning some of the core cultural and religious beliefs we all face, then continue to focus your intention on these issues and how you can continue to move forward.

More Loss

"Valerie, you better come quickly. She doesn't have much time left," Russ said in an urgent, apprehensive voice.

"I'll be right there, Russ." I hung up the phone knowing that the time I had anticipated and dreaded for so long had arrived. Sorrow overwhelmed me.

My dear friend, Lisa, had died of breast cancer.

I spoke at her funeral, overwhelmed with sadness and loss. I was angry and confused that God could have allowed such a beautiful being who never smoked or drank, and was an avid baseball player, loving mother, wife and friend, to be taken in her mid-forties.

Her death makes no sense to me.

Several times a week, Lisa and I would go on long walks for hours, talking and laughing about everything. She was a source of friendship, love, encouragement, and support in my life. She lived right up the street from me and it was always such a comfort to know she was always there if I needed her.

I miss you already, Lisa. I am so sorry...I love you so much. My heart was breaking with grief as I stared at the sunset while walking home from her house after she'd passed. It was the same street that we had walked so many times before. Tears of sadness streamed down my face as a warm blanket of love wrapped around me. I felt Lisa's spirit surrounding me in the beautiful sunset, and I was comforted by the gratitude of who she was and all that she meant to me.

Little did I know that more loss was around the corner...

The Worst Pain

"I stood here before you only six months ago, in the same church behind the same pulpit, to celebrate the life of my dear friend Lisa. It is unimaginable that I am now here once again, to offer the eulogy for my own daughter, Jessica."

Only six months after Lisa passed away, my first daughter, Jessica, passed away in her sleep. More than 350 people attended Jessica's funeral at the original church where I began my parent support group so many years earlier. My younger kids grew up going there while they were in grade school and Jessica also attended Sunday school there throughout her childhood and into her teens. She loved the church and I will always be so grateful that as a young mother, I had the support of this church community in my life. Jessica had many friends in the youth group and she loved the youth pastor. They were of great support during those teen years of turmoil when we received her diagnosis of bi-polar disorder.

She was diagnosed with ADHD when she was very young and continued to have challenges with an eating disorder in her teens. Later, she was diagnosed with bi-polar disorder and then a seizure disorder at seventeen.

Because of these issues, Jessica was a client of the Regional Center. As an adult, the Regional Center assisted Jessica with supported living services to learn the functional skills she needed to be successful with living on her own. I was highly involved in advocating for Jessica throughout her young adult years and prior to her moving away from home when she was trying to be an independent adult at the age of twenty-six.

As a child, Jessica was extremely creative and had a profound imagination as a result of being an only child until she was eleven when I had Chanel. She loved to sing, dance, and draw, and was adept at entertaining herself in the most amazing ways. When she was twelve, we began taking oil painting and figure-drawing classes together.

When Jessica decided to spread her wings as an adult and move away from home, our local Regional Center decided to discontinue her services. I was very upset with the fact that the Regional Center thought that Jessica no longer qualified for services. Without this support, Jessica was at risk of harm because she was not ready to be completely independent and without assistance from a service provider. At the time of her passing, I was in the middle of appealing the Regional Center's decision to discontinue services. I knew that Jessica needed these services, especially if she was going to be hundreds of miles away from me. I understood my daughter's desire to be independent and I respected her decision, but I wasn't about to allow another government agency to deny my child the services she required to be safe and healthy, especially if I could not be close to her.

The Regional Center

Many children who are on the autism spectrum are also clients of the California Regional Center where the qualifying disabilities for eligibility are Autism, Intellectually Impaired, Epilepsy, and Cerebral Palsy. The law that drives Regional Center services is the Lanterman Act. Regional Centers are nonprofit private corporations that contract with the Department of Developmental Services to provide or coordinate services and supports for individuals with developmental disabilities. They have offices throughout California to provide a local resource to help find and access the many services available to individuals and their families.

To be eligible for services, a person must have one of the qualifying disabilities that begins before the person's eighteenth birthday and be expected to continue indefinitely. Eligibility is established through diagnosis and assessment performed by Regional Centers.

Infants and toddlers (age 0 to 36 months) who are at risk of having developmental disabilities or who have a developmental delay may also qualify for services.

After Jessica's passing, I was shocked and horrified to find out that she had not been seeing a doctor or taking her seizure and bi-polar medication after she moved. Because the Regional Center discontinued her services, she was not assisted to get to the doctors office and be supervised for her medication needs.

Since the coroner's report stated that it was possible that she died from a seizure in her sleep or a possible heart attack, I felt that the Regional Center failed to do their job in meeting Jessica's needs and assisting her to be successful in independent living. If the Regional Center had continued to serve her, she would have been under a doctor's care and therefore, may have been treated for a possible heart condition and her seizures would have been under control.

Once again, my anger toward our broken system for individuals with disabilities was fueled. Because Jessica wanted to be independent and take care of herself, I had no idea that she was not seeing a doctor for her medical issues. This caused me to feel tremendous guilt and anger because if I had known, I would have addressed it. I couldn't help but wonder: *If Jessica had been under a doctor's care, it may have saved her life.*

After Jessica's sudden death, I felt as though everything in my life that served to stabilize me in the world was pulled out from under me. I had experienced so much loss and so quickly—the church community, my friend Lisa, and now Jessica. I was in a very dark place and, again, had to practice courage. Every day, I searched the tunnel of darkness to try and find a glimmer of light.

"Follow Your Heart, Mommy"

Will this pain ever stop? I sat in my bathroom on the little floral bench in front of my makeup table, tears of unspeakable sorrow streaming down my cheeks. I hardly recognized myself as I looked at my face lined with sadness and grief, my blue eyes dimmed. My once bright and young complexion was pale and vacant, adding at least ten years to my young middle-aged face. My blonde hair looked as if it had grayed and lost its luster overnight. My slim, upright body was exhausted and hunched over by the weight of the emotional pain of grief.

I felt lifeless, as if every emotion and ability to function had been sucked out of my body and mind by the vacuum of a mother's worst nightmare—the loss of her child. My heart felt as if it was actually breaking apart into shards of glass, causing my body to double over in pain as if I had been shot in the chest. Desperately, I grasped at my heart to somehow try and ease the suffering. I felt like a walking, hemorrhaging wound, and I had no idea how to begin to stop the bleeding.

It had been two weeks since my eldest daughter, Jessica, had passed away; and as I looked at my reflection in the mirror, I wondered, *How am I going to live another day with this tormenting grief...and this...burning emptiness? She was only twenty-eight years old. She had her whole life in front of her.*

The fact that the autopsy did not reveal an actual reason for her death made my agony even worse. The incessant questions continued to bombard my mind.

What really happened? Was it a seizure or a heart attack or neither? Why didn't I keep her with me? I shouldn't have put her on the bus to go back home after Christmas. I knew something was wrong that day, yet I still dropped her off and waved goodbye as the bus drove away. Maybe if she was home with me, I could I have done something to save her!

The shock and magnitude of losing a child without any kind of suspicion is unprecedented territory for any parent, and this was certainly the case for me. I was emotionally dead inside, like a walking zombie. I planned her funeral to meet the standard of what I thought would honor the life of my beautiful daughter. I seemed to remain strong and gracious throughout the ceremony, but the truth is I that I simply was not present at all. I was just going through the motions of daily life from the moment we received the unimaginable call from the coroner's office. The shock was just too great to actually accept or process mentally or emotionally.

I seemed to be fluctuating in a state of pure emotional chaos, as my feelings ran the gamut between numbness that left me detached from my body and confusion and disbelief in my mind. My life felt like a frightening rollercoaster of intense emotions that were completely out of my control.

I can't believe I will never see my daughter again. How is it possible that I will never hold her or be in her physical presence for the rest of my life here on this earth?

My mind once again argued with thoughts of impossible hope: *She isn't really gone, is she? She will call you tomorrow, Valerie. This isn't really happening. This must just be a bad dream.*

Oh my God! It is real! I knew I had to face the reality. *Jessica is gone and she's never coming back, and I will never see her or hold her again.* The finality of it all was simply too much to bear.

I glanced back at myself in the mirror and cried out to God for a lifeline in the midst of my agony. *God, please help me. Show me how to deal with this pain. I can't bear another day of this horrible uncontrollable grief.*

Suddenly, I felt a presence in the room and noticed complete and sheer silence, and the light in my bathroom seemed to brighten with a golden glow.

Wait, what is that?

I saw a pink shimmer of light turn the corner from my bedroom and move into my bathroom. Jessica's favorite color was pink.

My pain immediately dissipated, "Jessica!" I instantly knew it was my daughter's spirit. I can't explain how I knew, but I knew it was her spirit present in the room with me.

Is this real? Could this be an answer to my prayers and desperate calls for help? My heart was bursting with hope and anticipation. I was so excited and overwhelmed with awe at the thought of actually being able to connect with my beautiful daughter again.

A warm blanket of Jessica's essence and unimaginable peace and well-being poured over me. I closed my eyes, trying to allow myself to receive what she had come to communicate to me.

My heart heard her message during a conversation between our souls:

"Jessica, I love you. I miss you so much. I am so sorry that you died alone and that I wasn't there with you. I am so sad and I just can't bear this pain. I can't accept or understand why this happened and that I did not have the opportunity to say goodbye to you, to hold you and kiss you and tell you how much I love you along with all the things I would have said to you if I had known you were going to die. I don't want to be here without you. I want to be with you. I just can't bear this pain."

"Mommy," Jessica liked to call me Mommy even though she was twenty-eight years old. This was part of her sweet and innocent spirit that made her who she was. "I am okay, I am fine. I am with you. Please don't worry about me. Please don't be sad for me. I am alright and I am happy. This is what was meant to be for me. You need to understand this, and someday you will understand. You need to go on with your life. You have so much more work to do and so much love to offer to the world. You have so much more life to live and so much more to learn. It is not your time yet. There is so much more for you to do and be here on earth. There is a plan for you to fulfill on earth. Mommy… FOLLOW YOUR HEART."

"FOLLOW YOUR HEART." Those words rang the loudest and clearest out of all the words that were relayed to me in that soul communication I had with Jessica that day.

"Okay, Jessica. But I miss you." Almost as soon as I said the words, the intensity of her presence dissipated.

Her message made so much sense while she was there, but after she left, the message became unclear.

"Follow your heart" is such a pat answer. It suddenly seemed so trivial and contrived. I was so encouraged in the moment of Jessica's presence, but it seemed so meaningless to me when she was gone.

My grief and pain did not allow me to understand the deep meaning of Jessica's words. It certainly did not satisfy my need to know why she died or at least provide me with some sort of meaningful reason for her untimely death. Nevertheless, this message was auspiciously imprinted deep within my heart.

The Subject of Grief

My first reaction was to educate myself on the subject of "grief." I thought that if I gained the knowledge I needed to understand how to deal with this, I could quickly move through the darkness as fast as possible and I wouldn't have to fall apart. And so I began reading grief recovery books and easily learned all the head knowledge about the five steps of grief. I studied it online and went to the bookstore and bought five of the bestselling books on grief.

I actually thought that there was a chance that if I could learn what to do and understand how to get through this, I could be all right and make it through to the acceptance stage quickly. *I don't want to get depressed and be swallowed up in grief.* I was right in the middle of my victory of the systems reform, which made it even more difficult for me to feel the grief that I was so afraid to face.

Because I only learned the steps through intellectual knowledge and hadn't done the real experiential work through my heart, I continued to struggle with feelings of anger and frustration. *Why did this happen? What is wrong with the world? Where is God in all of this? Jessica went through so much as a teenager and young adult, why was her life cut short too?*

What continued to trigger my feelings of grief was the fact that when the "event" of her passing was over and everyone stopped calling, sending cards, and asking how I was doing, I was left alone to deal with my grief. This was when the real pain really sank in.

People move on with their lives and just expect you to do the same. I would become so irritated and incensed when I would receive the "pat" answers that people would so easily give me in order to avoid the unpleasant subject of death, especially, the death of a child.

- "God won't give you more than you can handle."
- "Don't get stuck in your grief."
- "Jessica is in a better place."
- "She was a Christian so you can rest assured in knowing she is in heaven."
- "God was protecting her from more pain in her life."
- "Everything happens for a reason."
- "Sometimes you just have to have faith and you won't get the answers until you get to heaven."

I interpreted these pat answers to be insensitive, as a simplistic offering to placate me. These responses were meaningless to me because I was living in a black hole.

Most people are at a loss for what to say or do to support a friend or loved one through a period of grief when the answer is really very simple: Just take the time to be there for them and give them permission to grieve. Allow them to talk about it and listen with an open heart. Without trying to fix them, say the words, "I am so sorry you are experiencing this grief, but I am here for you," and ask them what they would like you to do to offer your love and support.

Although it is quite tempting to simply use head knowledge or spiritual quotes and ideals as a quick fix to swiftly move through difficult times in life, it does not allow the opportunity to dig deep and experience the transformative evolution that these dark, tragic times offer to us in our human experience.

Losing a child feels like you have experienced an earthquake shaking you to the core, only the earthquake continues for many years after it began. Jessica's passing broke open all the pain of my childhood, all of the unprocessed grief of Chanel having autism, and all of the anger about the injustice of it all—the loss of my dear friend, feelings about my life not going the way I wanted it to, and doubting my spiritual foundation. Self-doubt bombarded my mind with questions about why these "tragedies" kept coming, which in turn fueled my confusion about why my religious beliefs were not providing me with real answers that resonated with my soul. As the times of loss and overwhelming grief continued to invade my life, I knew my only choice was to walk into the darkness and face my pain. I had to follow my heart, as Jessica had urged me to do.

With a humbled and pure heart, I set out on a spiritual quest to find the answers that I was so desperately seeking. I learned that there was a name for what I was facing: "The dark night of the soul." I knew that these are caused by a tragic event or loss of a loved one, which in turn brings about the collapse of what we believed to be true in life. What I didn't know was how to move through it to ultimately find the answers at the finish line.

No, pat answers will not do anymore. I need real answers and real tools to deal with all of this pain, grief, and uncertainty. If I don't do this work, I will be devoured by these feelings. With an unwavering determination, I set out to find a way to heal and get back to love.

And Chanel confirmed it repeatedly. She was always coming into my room to check on me, bringing me words of hope and healing, "Mom, Jessica doesn't want you to be sad. Jessica is fine, Mom. Don't you know? She doesn't want you to cry. Please Mom, you need to get over this... you need to heal yourself, Mom." At only fifteen years old, she was acting as a loving spiritual guide for me. This is so typical for many children with autism who are energetically sensitive and spiritual intuitives.

This work required me to be brutally honest with myself. I humbled myself and gathered all the courage I could muster daily to find the determination to walk through the darkness alone...to follow my heart when I could barely feel it. As I continued to learn to be responsible for my own life and aware of my authentic feelings, I was able to connect with the deep truths that were right for *me*.

Once again, I was not able to be fully present for my children in fulfilling my motherly duties. Because I was so deeply entrenched in moving through my "dark night of the soul," my husband filled in the gaps for me. Dealing with the loss of a child and processing the emotions of grief required everything I had within me. Looking back, it is still difficult for me not to feel guilty for missing so much of my children's young lives. I have had many discussions about this time with my children as adults, and they assure me that they were fine and not to let it bother me. But as a mother, I missed out on precious memories that cannot be replaced. I have come to forgive myself in knowing that I did the best I could at the time in balancing my own healing and my role as a mother.

I began studying Yoga with a local gym and fell in love with the practice. What an amazing way to release stress and physical and emotional pain that had been hurting my body, mind, and soul. I was drawn to how it is not only a mind/body connection but also a spiritual practice. After practicing at least three times a week for several years, I began attending a yoga studio and took the Teacher Training to delve deeper.

As part of this community, I followed my heart to India and stayed thirty days in an ashram in 2011. This was a tremendous experience of healing and restoration for me. I practiced Yoga, I ate extremely healthy food, and I spent a lot of time working through the intense grief of Jessica's death as well as meditating on my calling as an advocate. This experience helped me bring into focus the areas in my life that I needed to work on and gave me the courage to be bitterly honest with myself. Being exposed to a new way of thinking about religion awakened me to the wonder of creating my own personal way to experience God.

I was beginning to understand that we all have a choice about how we respond to the circumstances of our lives, and take responsibility for where we are on our path in life.

I thought I had been doing that, especially with Chanel, but Jessica's death propelled me into a whole new level of accepting my responsibility for my own life and learning to love myself the way Chanel had taught me to love. With Jessica as the catalyst, I was learning to live inclusively with non-polarity…the whole experience of being human and the opportunity it provides us to know ourselves.

By not running away from the dark times in my life, I began learning how to move through the evolutionary process of learning how to live in this life with a sense of wholeness and connection to all of humanity and our beautiful planet. Chanel's diagnosis, Lisa's passing, and Jessica's passing actually caused me to expand my faith from the rules of organized religion to non-judgment and freedom, opening me up to see that every experience in my life has actually been a gift to continue to move me forward in knowing myself fully, learning to speak my own truth, and doing what I am here to do on the planet.

Two years later, I got yet another opportunity to practice love.

Will It Ever Stop?

"How are you doing, Valerie?" my friend asked me at a dinner party.

"Well the truth is I am really tired of working from morning until late into the night to try and keep our head above water and just make the bills to stay in the house,"

I said, knowing my voice was taught with exhaustion and frustration. "It has really been a struggle for the children and for me since Michael lost the business and we lost the lifestyle we once knew."

My friends comment was, "Well, you gotta do what you gotta do!"

Here we go again with another "pat" answer. Needless to say, this is not what I wanted to hear. I already knew how to do what I had to do…I had been doing that all my life. I was proficient at remaining strong in a crisis and surviving on my own. What I really wanted and needed was some empathy and encouragement at a time I was feeling so discouraged and disappointed with what was going on in my life. Once again, I felt as if my friends and family were insensitive and indifferent to how hard this was for me.

Today, I know that most of the time, people just simply don't know what to say, so they throw out the "pat" answer. Some just don't know how to show or feel empathy because they feel as though their life is hard too. Many others just cannot relate because they haven't experienced something like it themselves so they aren't able to give words of encouragement. What I really needed and wanted to hear was, "Valerie, I am so sorry you are going through this right now, but you know there is some lesson in this for you and you know that you will learn it when you are ready."

Chanel's answer was much more loving. She came in to check in with me regularly. "Mom, is everything alright?" Or she would give me words of encouragement, "Mom, everything will work out fine, don't worry." She was always pointing out how beautiful life was by talking about dogs or showing me the latest rose that had bloomed in the garden. "Look, look, Mom! The moon is so full and so bright! Wow, it's amazing!" Chanel was connected to everything in the universe and she deeply felt its beauty. She was my constant reminder, calling me back to love.

As I contemplated my financial situation and the stress my anger was putting on my marriage and me, I remembered what Chanel's life and Jessica's passing had taught me about love. *I cannot push this pain and frustration away and expect things to get better. I have to find the lesson in all of this. And so, I continued to peel the onion as life continued to strip me of all that was not love.*

Marital Stress

Marital stressors for parents of children with disabilities are only exacerbated when coupled with life's typical marriage issues. Because of this, most couples are pushed to the brink of divorce.

Statistics show that 85% of marriages of children with special needs end in divorce. It is amazing that Michael and I are still married after all we have been through. I'm not even going to get into the issues we had with our other two younger teenagers! Agreeably, it is extremely difficult to remain together through life's typical challenges and stressors, but when you add a special needs child into the mix (and many families have two special needs children), the odds of a marriage lasting are stacked against them. To add to our marital stress, Michael and I were not only dealing with parenting children with special needs, our marriage was also challenged with a serious financial blow in 2008 and then the death of our child.

These are the stressors I hear about most often from my clients:

- A husband falls short in supporting the wife in the responsibility of advocating for the child's education, which in turn, causes the wife to feel resentment.
- Financial hardships.
- Grief (denial, anger, depression) over the diagnosis.
- Siblings acting out because most of the attention is focused on the special needs child.
- Physical and emotional burnout, due to juggling so many responsibilities.

I want to make a very important point here: when we are experiencing problems in our marriage and are unhappy, so are our children, especially autistic children. And our children will mirror the conflicts of our inner life.

I knew Chanel, and both my other children as well, were feeling my unfulfilled ideals. I was conditioned to believe that happiness and prosperity were achieved by financial and marital success, and it was very painful to be in conflict with myself as I reluctantly contemplated whether or not to end my marriage.

But in my mind, I would argue with myself, *How could you break up the family unit? I can't do this to my children... this will break their hearts.*

I fluctuated back and forth, trying to make a decision about divorce for several years. Getting a divorce was against everything I had believed as a Christian. *How could I make a decision that would put my children through that kind of suffering?*

My family meant everything to me. Being together as a family unit meant everything to me. As a child, it was what I had always wanted—a true family, which included a home, my children, and a husband that loved and provided for his family. You see, that was *not* my childhood experience. I did not have security, safety and parents that remained married. So, the state of my marriage was another dream shattered. Another ideal disassembled in my life. But I could not ignore my discontentment and the challenges in my marriage. Because I had to be truthful and honest with myself, I learned how to transmute my belief system to function within my marriage with integrity and authenticity.

Whether a marriage ends or doesn't end is not the issue here. Letting go of the things that do not support us in our own evolution is. Just as I learned that it is possible to be "called away" from a calling, there are also times when a marriage relationship can be "completed." We don't have to view it as a relationship that has failed but instead see it as the relationship has come to completion. No judgment. Not good or bad.

I was finally learning that I would not find the answers I was so desperately seeking by looking outside myself. My answers could not be dependent on the explanations of others' conceptual beliefs or my illusionary identity. I was in the process of awakening to a deeper sense of purpose and connectedness with a greater life and true understanding of myself.

Throughout the turmoil, Chanel's beautiful presence was a constant resonance of love that continued to shine bright within our family. When Michael and I would fight, she would reprimand us with words of wisdom, "Mom, Dad, you need to love each other and stop this fighting. We need to be a family. Please, we need to stop this arguing. We are a family!"

Her high expectations and radiant countenance kept me pushing onward to believe that this was an evolutionary process, both for my family and me.

Do It For Your Angel

What challenges are you facing in your life? Are you reevaluating relationships in your life or are you struggling in your marriage? Are you experiencing financial hardships? Is your faith being challenged? Are you aware of the thoughts that your inner critic speaks to you about this situation? What old hurts and feelings have been triggered as a result of this time of adversity? Have you considered the possibility that this affliction could serve as a vehicle to heal those childhood wounds that have been exposed?

I was trying to navigate through the myriad of unanswered questions about Jessica's death, my advocacy journey, my spiritual transition, and now our financial crisis. It felt like one blow after another, but I now know that life was taking every opportunity to show me how to heal myself. It seemed so wrong at the time, but I see it all so clearly now. This was another open door to allow me to see and feel and heal old hurts from my childhood, revise religious beliefs that just didn't make sense, and embrace the message of love that our children offer to us as the parent of a special needs child.

Through it all, Chanel's presence in our family was the glue that held us all together. Her love and angelic innocence and purity gave our family the hope that we needed to keep moving forward through these times of grief and loss. When I felt as if I couldn't take any more pain, Chanel's message of love gave me the hope I needed to believe that there was a purpose for all of it. Whether it was dealing with the discrimination, the grief, and the marital and financial stressors that accompany a child with special needs, or facing the death of my beautiful daughter, Jessica, Chanel's amazing energy of love and compassion brought me through it all. With each loss, I became more aware of my internal intuitive guidance system. This new awareness allowed me to recognize old paradigms or "stories" as false belief systems that just did not work anymore and were holding me back from standing in my power and speaking my own truth.

Throughout this pivotal time, Chanel was helping me move from Depression to Acceptance, and I was on my way to understanding the true reason for all of this…

"When she transformed into a butterfly, the caterpillars spoke not of her beauty, but of her weirdness. They wanted her to change back into what she always had been. But she had wings."

Dean Jackson

CHAPTER 5

ANGEL GIFTS

As I rushed into the school, my heart was pounding. I was late picking up Chanel from high school. My eyes scanned the front office, but Chanel and her aide were not there. My stomach began to tighten. I called for the assistant principal to see if she knew where they might be. She didn't have any information and got on the walkie-talkie to contact security and found out the aide had left Chanel alone in the front office because I was late.

The security guards scoured the entire school campus, but Chanel was nowhere to be found. Now I was sick to my stomach and the fear began to escalate. I called my husband who quickly headed over to help with the search and called his brothers to assist. We put a call into the police to start hunting for Chanel throughout the neighborhood. As I watched everyone start the search, my body began to shake and I doubled over with nausea. *Valerie, don't faint! You have to find her!*

Almost ninety minutes had passed since the bell rang and there was still no sign of Chanel. We had called our friends and family and everyone was praying for her safe return. I could not imagine where she could be. *Was she kidnapped? Did some boy from the high school coerce her into leaving with him?*

Suddenly, my brother-in-law asked, "Have you checked your house? Maybe she walked home?"

"No, she would never do that! She has never walked home before and she knows that I pick her up every day." I could not imagine Chanel doing something so out of character, but my brother-in-law sprinted to his car and drove to our house, hoping he would find Chanel there, safe and sound.

Sure enough, we got the call: "Chanel is sitting on your front porch waiting for you guys! She asked why it was taking you so long to get home! Oh yeah, and she said she got the mail from the mailbox for you too," he said with a chuckle in his voice.

We raced home and I pulled her into a desperate hug. I was so relieved to see her…she was safe…she was home. "Chanel, honey, you know you are suppose to wait for me in the office! We were so worried about you! Why did you do that, Chanel?"

"Mom, I am a big girl now. I am in high school! I can take care of myself and I can walk home by myself. I know the way, Mom! Please Mom, you need to trust me!" Chanel stated with confidence. But I could see her frustration bubbling with my clear lack of understanding of her desire to be independent.

I realized that day that Chanel was perfectly capable of taking care of herself and that I needed to stop being so overprotective of her as well as more focused on fostering her independence. That day, Chanel *showed* me in a very BIG way, that I needed to trust her and that she wanted to be treated like any other high school girl her age. Yes, this was a hard lesson that was very traumatic for me, but it was the way Chanel communicated how much she needed me to accept her for who she really was. It was the only way she knew how to *show* me because she did not have the ability to communicate her frustration with words.

Sometimes, acceptance is right there, staring us in the face, but we are so afraid of it that we choose to remain in fear. Fear of the unknown, fear of what might happen if we let go, fear of trusting God and the universe and, most importantly, fear of trusting our child and their own intuition. I knew that I had to really work on trusting Chanel and letting go of my fear and control in every situation so I could feel that she was safe. That day, I had an AHA moment that my overprotectiveness was all about me giving myself the assurance that Chanel was safe rather than allowing Chanel to grow in her own independence.

That day, I stepped a little deeper into the acceptance stage in the journey of a special needs parent. That day, I realized that Chanel was growing up just like every other teen grows up when they are in high school.

I believe this phase is extremely important for every parent with a special needs child. Regardless of what others have said about their capacity, or the fears in our own heart of what may happen, the question is this: How can we truly accept these children for who they are and respect them for what they are here to do?

Possibilities and Hope

I was "called to" work with families of children with special needs and that calling spoke to me through one daughter's autism and another daughter's death.

I had to write this book to help you look further, past the label and disability, to listen to your heart, and then learn to follow it. You, too, can advocate for your angel, change the way you look at your marriage, improve your financial situation, and find answers to some of your toughest existential questions. You can do it if you learn to trust yourself.

Life gives us possibilities.

We have the choice to view our children's disability and all the challenges they have brought into our life as a problem…or as a gift. When we begin to think differently about our child's disability, look at the big picture of what they are teaching us, and become aware of what they have already taught us, we begin to feel the hope that we've been seeking.

I wrote this book to give you hope. Whether you are in the depths of despair, victim thinking, isolation, fear, frustration, or questioning your faith or your child's future, I wrote this book to help open you up to the possibilities that are endless for you and your child. I want to challenge you to think about the "big picture" and see how things will work together for good…if you make the decision to choose to look at them as teachers. I hope that, in reading this book, you have been given the passion to empower yourself with the knowledge and advocacy skills that you need to meet the educational needs of your individual child.

And…there is another large component to meeting the needs of your special needs child.

Angel Energy

I believe your child is here for an even larger purpose. You have an angel living in your home. Take a deep breath and move into your heart and feel how your life has changed since your child was born. Look past the struggle and the stress, the battle with the school district, the hours of research in trying to educate yourself, the fights with your spouse, the sleepless nights worrying about the choices you were facing, and the tears of grief that you have shed, and ask yourself these questions…

What is the energy that your child brings into your home? How do you feel when you are with your child? Do you feel as though you are in the moment and all other things melt away? Do they bring you into the Now, where all the noise in your head stops and you can just "be?"

Anyone you talk to will tell you that there is something very special about these kids. Sensitive and caring service providers, teachers, friends, relatives, and parents alike all say that they are such gentle beings and live in their own special reality. I have heard story after story about how an autistic child has enriched their life and made them a more loving and caring person.

These kids are powerful energetic agents of change, and it is our job to open our eyes and see them for who they truly are and then open our hearts to what they came here to do.

Chanel is only one child, and the ripple of change that she has created within our own family and the lives of others is unimaginable!

Angel Communication and Intuition

Think about how you speak to your child. Do you communicate with your child sometimes without words? Do you feel as though they can read your mind? They don't really need words because they have the capacity to communicate without them. These kids are intuitives! This is how they operate naturally. They sense and feel everything on an energetic level. While most of us have to learn to listen to our intuition when it speaks to us (because we were taught to discount our feelings at an early age in our culture), the autistic population knows that their intuition is their most trustworthy guide and the only way of existence that they know.

This means that they can see through our counterfeit attempts to communicate through our body language or words. It's as if they can see right through to the authenticity of our hearts about what we are feeling and thinking. We try and speak to them with words that have nothing to do with how we are really feeling, but our insincere attempts to communicate send our children mixed messages. No matter how hard we try to persuade them to buy into the illusion that nothing is wrong, they know the truth.

Angel Purpose

Why do you think they react the way they do and have the "behavioral difficulties" that they exhibit? My first, more clinical, answer to this is that they are trying to communicate their discomfort—too much noise, or light, or activity. But my second, and more intuitive, answer is that they are also trying to teach us to live and communicate more authentically. They are trying to get us to quiet our minds of all the noise and be in the present moment where peace and unconditional love have the power to heal lives.

For those who can open their hearts and minds to a paradigm shift and accommodate the uniqueness of these children, they will be blessed by the presence and unconditional love that these angels can bring into our lives. For those who are unable to see them as exceptional and not less than, life can look like a hostile battlefield for all concerned.

Do It for Your Angel

Try an exercise with your child. Sit with them and just breathe. First, take three deep cleansing breaths, and then try and match your breath to the breath of your child. Soon your child will be breathing with you in harmony. Clear your mind and focus on your harmonic breath. You can close your eyes, or not, hold your child's hand, or not... whatever your child leads you to do. Your child will lead you *if* you decide to be open to their lead. They are our teachers, and they will love doing this or any kind of exercise that will allow them to just "be" with you.

These moments of being present together with your child will begin to lift the veil that blocks us from seeing the possibilities in our kids.

One Angel's Impact

"Mrs. Barretto (name has been changed for confidentiality), Mat does not require the support of a special education classroom any longer. He can now be fully included in a general education classroom," the special education teacher proudly proclaimed to the parent and the IEP team.

During our last IEP meeting when the Special Education teacher gave her victorious proclamation to the team, we sat around the IEP table and reminisced about how far we had come, marveling at Mat's progress. Each and every service provider, educator, and administrator took their turn as they described their experience of love, pride, and gratitude in being a part of this success story. Many shared how Mat has changed the way in which they view kids with autism and how he has enriched their lives and the lives of the children in his general education classroom.

Mrs. Barretto relayed her gratitude and appreciation to her "Dream Team" (as she has fondly named Mat's IEP team) through tears of joy and awe. This is true success—this is what we all strive to achieve for all special needs children.

Five years earlier, Mat's parents hired me to speak on their behalf. The school district was not serving Mat and the parents were beside themselves with worry and anxiety about their son's future. Mat was on the spectrum. He wasn't talking and was not receiving any services other than being placed in a special education classroom. Mat's autism caused him to hold his ears and scream. Unable to communicate, he could not take direction from the teacher, and his parents were unable to take him outside the home without Mat having tantrums and meltdowns.

Mat's parents flew to the Philippines, back to their home, to have Mat evaluated and to receive speech and language services.

"Are you kidding me?" I was appalled that these parents actually flew their child to the Philippines to receive speech services. "You don't have to do that, Mr. and Mrs. Barretto! That is the most outrageous thing I have heard yet from one of my clients…Wow." I was somewhere between shocked with disbelief and incensed with anger about the injustice of it all. "Don't worry, we are going to get Mat all the services he needs. I can also tell you that Mat will be mainstreamed into a general education classroom and our ultimate goal is to have him fully included in a general education classroom before he reaches Junior High."

Now I don't make this prediction to every parent, but Mat was different. I only say this to parents when I can speak those words with complete conviction that there is a very good chance that this will actually happen. It was a knowing I had in my gut about Mat—the same knowing I had with my own daughter Chanel.

My prediction was correct. That is exactly what happened for Mat. But this victory did not come without a price that was laden with pain, hard work, and perseverance.

This was the beginning of the "change over" in the school district, so we were fervently opposed when we first began conducting IEP meetings for Mat. It took more than a year before I finally had developed the supports and services with appropriate goals. It was a very rocky road because his parents only saw the intense resistance from the district meeting after meeting and it sometimes looked as if nothing was happening. I kept reassuring his parents that we were developing the evidence to support our requests for services and that eventually they would be receiving the program they had dreamed about for their son.

I gave hours and hours of parent training to this mother, Mrs. Barretto. I would explain to her what I was doing and why I was doing it so she could understand the IEP process. We held meeting after meeting in order to show the evidence that Mat needed an intensive Speech and Language program, a private ABA full-time aide, an intensive ABA program, and Occupational Therapy. Over the years, he has continued to receive intensive services such as three hours a week of private speech and language and also a program to address auditory processing called "Fast Forward" that was provided through a private agency. Mat was also provided a private ABA agency with a one-on-one behavioral aide.

Many times, Mat's parents were tempted to give up under the pressure of the battle, the financial obligation for my services, and the length of time it took to receive services and see a positive change in their son. But because these parents held onto their dreams and their faith in me as an advocate, Mat will enter junior high as a *general education* student. And even more exciting, Mat no longer exhibits the characteristics of autism and is able to access grade level curriculum.

Not only has Mat's mother grown immensely over the years because of this, but he has also enriched the lives of so many people. Every one of them speak about how their involvement with Mat has given them an experience of love, faith, and pure amazement. He was the glue that brought this IEP team together to work in solid collaboration, putting aside their own egos and uniting in one goal to see Mat fully included in general education. Special education can work beautifully, when it is done with the true intention of IDEA and gives permission to these special angels to accomplish their purpose here on earth.

This is the magic of special needs children. When people have the willingness to be open-minded enough to let go of their personal opinions, limiting low expectations, and fear-based rules, special needs children can be our greatest teachers.

The Paradigm Shift

What if millions of autistic individuals are here to teach us a different way of living that will lead us to be more deeply connected so we can ultimately live with unconditional love that this world hasn't seen before? Have you noticed that autistics are not driven by their personalities and egos? They do not care about materialism or the latest fashion. They live in a world of connection, bliss, and truthfulness. They do not know how to be anything else.

Is this a disorder or a blessing? Must we see it as something we should "cure," or something we can learn from?

I believe they are the pebble that is dropped in the body of water to create ripples of endless change to support the shift in raising the consciousness of the planet.

Many times, the challenges we encounter with our child happen when we try to impose our rules of what acceptable and appropriate behavior looks like, as defined by the regulations and limitations of our agreed upon society because they can feel our emotions and they reflect their environment. These are the times when our kids' behaviors will escalate. If you, as a parent, can let go of that thinking of "how things are suppose to be," and simply practice *being* with your child by allowing the moment to unfold, you will begin your journey of possibilities with your autistic child. Learn to know your child for who they really are, complete with amazing wisdom and many unique gifts that they are bringing into your life.

One day, when Michael and I were in line at the grocery store, arguing about money, Chanel stepped between us and put her hands out toward both of us in protest. "Mom, Dad, please stop! Please, you must stop this arguing. You must love each other!"

Be aware of what you say in front of your child regardless of whether they are verbal or non-verbal. They are taking in everything, whether you think so or not. When there is dissension in the home, they can feel it and will react to it in their "autistic" way. Your child will reflect your thoughts, emotions, and behaviors back to you like a mirror, triggering the emotions and exact areas in your life that need healing.

That is their job as an angel in your family.

Your child will lead you if you let them. Chanel was non-verbal (except for echolalia) until she was eight years old. Now, at twenty-four, she recalls experiences, places, and events in great detail, back to when she was four years old.

Our kids know exactly what we are saying and are fully present, even if they don't "appear" to be paying attention or communicating in a way that we call "normal." When Chanel was seven and we would be driving in the car, she would point which way to turn to get to our destination; that is how present and aware she was and still is. Chanel has better sense of direction than I do, I can tell you that for sure!

Angel Mirrors

Our children will help us to heal ourselves. They will assist us to become more authentic and let go of thinking that no longer serves us. They are our never-ending reminders to continue to peel the onion. They will teach us how to love ourselves and assist us to truly know ourselves on our journey of self-discovery. The greatest gift you can give them is to be aligned to yourself—body, mind and soul.

Parents, I am not implying that your child is reflecting your areas of wounding only. They are probably reflecting back some really beautiful parts as well—your true self, your courage, your perseverance, and your ability to love them unconditionally. The parent/child relationship is reciprocal and therefore, we are working together with our children to learn a new way of communicating and being in this world.

In learning how to communicate with our special child, we are learning the ability to be self-aware and how to be present in the moment. As we move through the hustle and bustle of our work schedules, along with the demands of our children's therapies and remedial special education programs and the stress that our daily lives can bring, we can easily forget the importance of connecting with our child. We move from one responsibility to another without being fully present with our child. With a little practice, and as you learn self-awareness, you will begin to learn how to be present in the moment. Being present will change your child's behavior. Try it, test it…. and see the positive effect it can have on your child.

A good place to start is for you, as the parent, to create the space to allow your child to show you their full potential without feeling the need to control the outcome or the need to have all the answers. As we honor our child by being fully present, our child becomes more communicative to better reflect our underlying issues in which we can provide healing for ourselves and for our children. The key for parents is to raise our own awareness and consciousness so that we are more able to meet our kids exactly where they are, right here, right now.

Whether your child is non-verbal or verbal, they are communicating all the time. When they exhibit what we might consider inappropriate behavior, they are communicating. If they use echolalia to repeat words or phrases, they are communicating something relative to the situation. If they make noises such as pops, clicks or sounds the vibration of that sound is also communication.

Listen and pay attention to how they are communicating. Feel what they are trying to express instead of dismissing their behavior as inappropriate because it doesn't look like the communication you want to see from them. The more you acknowledge, embrace, and respect their forms of communication, they, in turn, will be more willing to engage and interact to try and connect with you. And the communication between you and your child will grow.

Do It for Your Angel

Evaluate perceptions in your life that produce the emotions of anger, fear, resentfulness, and hopelessness. Honestly look at what feelings your child triggers in you and how you react to those triggers. Are your reactions moving you toward fear or love? When your child communicates in an unusual way, how do you feel? When your child throws a tantrum or has a meltdown in front of others, how do you feel? How can you transform these moments into an experience full of love and acceptance for your child and yourself?

Showering Acceptance

I used to view anyone who denied services to children as "*the enemy.*" For many years, I held anger toward those who did not believe that students should be provided with therapy, supports, or services. Yet this belief that I held only served to promote the "*us against them*" mentality.

Upon hearing their ridiculous reasons for not providing services, my blood would begin to boil and my heart would begin to feel as if it was going to pound out of my chest. I would have to purposefully concentrate on keeping my composure in order to respond appropriately with an appeal to their routine denial of services.

How can these people say this and sleep at night? Why did they become therapists and educators if they don't want to provide services to children? What kind of people would do this to a beautiful special angel child in need of these services?

After working for so many years with many of the same people from district to district, I see them as just people doing their jobs. I don't agree with them, and I wouldn't be able to do their job because I wouldn't be able to deny services to children who need them; but in their hearts, many of them truly believe that they are doing the right thing. They are not bad people, they are just people on their path, doing the best they can with what they know.

I am not denying the fact that some of these individuals use their position as a way to disguise areas of wounding and use it as a defense mechanism by abusing their power and authority, but our responsibility is to take the drivers seat for our own child's education by becoming an educated, knowledgeable advocate for our child. We have the power to change the outcome of our child's education and we will not give away that power by allowing the insecurities, opinions, or beliefs of others to delay or deny our children the education they deserve and require.

Again, Chanel's message of unconditional love, acceptance, and inclusion shines through, and I am finally learning to apply it in my life.

As an advocate today, I approach the IEP with the intention of *working together* in cooperation by building a collaborative team *instead of fighting for* what the child needs. Holding the space of accepting that everyone comes with different feelings, beliefs, information, and opinions… and that's okay.

You, too, can be working in acceptance and cooperation in building your team rather than in competition, which tears down and diminishes the flow and effectiveness of your team and ultimately jeopardizes meeting the needs of your child. When you interact with a team member by seeing them as a person who should be treated with respect and non-judgment instead of believing they are the enemy, the trajectory of your IEP meetings will change drastically.

One Advocate's Impact

"I am so afraid that I am doing the wrong thing for my child." Katherine took a deep breath before continuing to talk about her six-year-old autistic son. "I fluctuate back and forth with my decision. The Program Specialist tries to scare me by telling me that Brandon won't do well in an SDC classroom rather than the 'Severely Handicapped Autism Classroom,'" she explained with apprehension and fear in her voice.

"Katherine, we have discussed this so many times. I urge you to read about LRE and inclusion so you will be knowledgeable enough to stand upon your decision and accept what your child really needs. You have seen how much Brandon has progressed in the small amount of mainstreaming he has had in the SDC and General Education classroom. He is going into first grade and has already had two years in the *autism classroom*. He is so bright and intelligent and does not require a placement for severely handicapped children," I reiterated to her for the umpteenth time and tried to remain encouraging.

As an advocate, I spend hours of teaching time with parents of special needs children. I give sound legal advice, but parents must do whatever it takes for them to become strong and assured in the decisions that they make for their children, both in their minds and in their hearts. Acceptance can only be reached if we do the work in order to achieve that level of trust in our children and ourselves.

"I would have never known what to do if we had not found out about you, Valerie. I could have never had the courage to do this if you weren't there to support me." Her voice was full of gratitude and appreciation as she searched for the right words to relay how much I had helped her to find the answers, direction, and recommendations she was searching for her son.

"Well, Katherine, you are another pioneer mom who is paving the way for your district staff and other parents. It is not acceptable for them to continue to place children with the diagnosis of autism in an 'autism classroom.' This is a dinosaur mentality considering how far we have come with LRE and autism. You should be proud of yourself and feel honored that you have the courage to hold this district accountable in what they see as 'the norm' in their way of educating children on the spectrum. By taking the first step, you are opening the door to the possibilities for other parents to do the same. You are beginning to accept your role as a mother of a child with autism, with the courage to speak your truth and inspire others."

"Oh my gosh, Valerie! I have never thought of myself in that way! That is so exciting and unbelievable to me...I could never have done this without you."

"I am so happy for you, Katherine! That is my job—to empower you to advocate and inspire you, so you can then begin to lead others."

I see our role as parents as ambassadors of evolution, but our children are the ones who are the spiritual sages leading the way. Instead of a revolution (as I once fought for) we are assisting in the evolution of how society, education, and the medical realm perceive and relate to our children. These children challenge our family and social structure by compelling us to reflect on our feelings about diversity and equality, and then hold on to what we believe is right and equal and fair treatment of every living being.

They have caused medicine to review the safety of vaccines. The psychological realm has developed an entire new theory of behavioral intervention because of students on the spectrum. Autistics have caused education to become more inclusive-minded and create a whole new way of teaching by creating a system that educates children with special needs along side typical developing peers.

These special angels of change have challenged us to expand our minds and our perceptions to discover new ways of thinking with unlimited possibilities for humanity. If we are willing to be open to the possibilities, this shift can affect every aspect of our lives—political, social, and economic structures, as well as our environment, our work, and how we experience our relationships. We can recalibrate every thought we think and every feeling we have by transforming our perceptions of good and bad or right and wrong. Their ripple of change can awaken our awareness of who we really are and how to lead a more aligned life.

Both my daughters have influenced my life in ways that are far beyond what I would have ever dreamed as a young mother. Both, I consider to be angels in my life.

As Wayne Dyer says, "If we change the way we look at things, the things we look at change." I did not know the power and magnitude of this truth until I was brave enough to make the journey to find out what it could actually mean for me in my own life as I faced and learned to accept the diagnosis of autism and the loss of a child. Throughout this journey, Chanel was there waiting for me to listen, waiting for me to learn her auspicious lessons of love.

May you also have the courage and determination to find out what it can mean for you in your own life, as well as your role in the special needs community.

Are You an Imaginal Cell?

Out of your experience of being the parent of a special needs child, do you envision a world that accepts, supports, and includes your child without having them respond with fear based reactions and bureaucratic double-talk? Have you imagined changes that need to occur to allow your special needs child an opportunity to become the highest expression of themselves, without being labeled, segregated, and limited by social, educational and political norms? Have you tried to make a difference by pointing out these areas to family, friends and IEP team members, only to have them shut you down with their fear and resistance to shift away from the status quo? Do you feel like you are all alone in your attempts to be the ambassador of inclusion, acceptance, and unconditional love?

Consider these visions as "imaginary cells" within you that can give you the power to make those huge leaps of change.

The imaginal cell is how nature transforms the caterpillar into the butterfly during what we call metamorphosis. These imaginal cells are so completely different from the original caterpillar cells that the caterpillar cells think they are a virus or enemy and will begin attacking the imaginal cells. However, even though the imaginal cells are treated as outcasts for *not fitting in*, they still keep showing up as they continue to grow in numbers. Eventually, the imaginal cells begin to find each other and form a community. This new community of imaginal cells eventually becomes the creative program in transforming the caterpillar into the butterfly!

As a parent of a special needs child, I immediately was given the intuition, or you could call it "the imaginal cell," which served as a quiet whisper in my heart to believe that somehow, someway, I could make huge changes in myself to become less like the caterpillar and more like the butterfly. I was not willing to allow my caterpillar cells or the collective caterpillar cells of our society, the school district, or the church, to kill off my imaginal cells, which held the possibility for my daughter and my own transformation.

When I advocated for Chanel to be fully included in a general education classroom in 1997, I knew that I was meant to be one of the very first imaginal cells in my own school district. Even though they thought I was a virus and tried to make me extinct, I knew that I was meant to survive. Being one of the first imaginal cells to exist was a painful and lonely way to travel. But soon after, other imaginary cells just like me began to gather and, eventually, a community of imaginal cells was formed. Eventually, we morphed into a beautiful butterfly in the form of changing the outcomes of many children's lives and creating a positive systems reform in my own local school district.

Oh yes, and my own daughter, Chanel, the one that the developmental pediatrician's at UCLA said would never talk, read, or write…graduated with a high school diploma…with *honors*.

Sometimes in life, we are chosen to play the role of the imaginal cell in our own little community. Even though this can be a frightening undertaking at first, eventually others begin to join in the cause. The masses assume that we must be the enemy because why else would we be so different?

Today, the inclusion movement is the only viable option. How can we continue to serve special needs children in segregated classrooms when the numbers continue to rise at such an alarming rate? Will half the classes at our school sites be filled with kids with autism, ADHD, learning disabilities, and other neurological disorders while the other half be filled with classrooms full of the typical developing children?

Our children deserve a chance to reach their full potential in life by honoring their inalienable rights and personal freedom. Placing ceilings of disheartening predictions upon them is unethical and unjust, and destroys a parent's hope that their child will someday have an independent life.

You will know if you are one of us—an imaginal cell that was meant to grow and join together with like-minded community members. You, too, will need to fight your way out of the cocoon of self-doubt and rise above the opinions of polarity and judgment to claim your wings of freedom for yourself and your special needs child.

You will feel the call to your own personal metamorphosis as you step into your power to change into a new version of yourself. Your imaginal cells will inspire and challenge you. They will continue to gather together, creating possibilities for change to create something completely different for your life and the life of your child.

Just as I walked alone in the dark during many seasons of metamorphosis, you too may feel alone and unsure of what the future holds. But like mine, your fear can become your energy to seek out others who are like-minded imaginal cells to cluster together and form your community base for growth and transformation.

I will tell you to hold true to what you imagine for your child and to never give up. I will tell you to never allow anyone to discourage you from making your dreams for your child a reality. As you dedicate yourself to this great service for your child and to the world, you will be the recipient of great love in return. In dedicating ourselves to our children's message of unconditional love and acceptance, we will be the fortunate participants in creating change.

You hold the power to create what it is you want in your own life and determine the outcome of your child's education. You are the imaginal cell in your family, in your community, in your church, and in your local school district. The choices you make in your life and the decisions you choose for your special angel truly do make a difference in the evolution of our world today. These children are true angels of change. They may be misunderstood, ostracized, labeled less than and broken, yet they appeal to us to recognize what is no longer working and what was never actually true. These special angels deserve our tender loving care and devotion in supporting them to fulfill their purpose for being here.

Because of Chanel, and the unconditional love she brought into my life, I was given the opportunity to create a career that I would have never dreamed of choosing, which brought me the financial security and sense of achievement that I had always longed for. As a young adult in my twenties, I would have never believed that someday

I would have the career of a successful entrepreneur with my own educational advocacy niche. This work has transformed my life, cultivating such deep gratitude to have the privilege to be a part of the lives of these special angels. The opportunity to help these families in crisis and encourage them to believe that it is possible for their child to reach their full potential in life makes Chanel's presence a never-ending blessing.

Chanel's presence has facilitated change in my life, my spiritual path, and how I function within my marriage. She was the reason that I became a non-attorney advocate and found victory in my mission to create a system reform in my own local school district. She is the reason I wrote this book along with my beautiful daughter, Jessica, who was the catalyst that gave me the courage and motivation to *"follow my heart"* no matter what the cost.

Just think, if only one child, my daughter Chanel, could have caused the great amount of change that she has created because I followed her lead, how much evolution can the autistic population create as a collective if all parents would be willing to become the imaginal cell?

There are many others who agree and stand with us and who are inspired by our ability to learn from these special angels who continue to come into our world every day. Together, we can honor the truth in their undeniable message of acceptance and unconditional love.

Will you have the courage to help your angel find their wings?

"Who you are is so much more than what you do.

The essence, shining through the heart, soul, and center,

the bare and bold truth of you does not lie in your to-do list.

You are not just at the surface of your skin,

not just the impulse to arrange the muscles of your face into a smile or a frown,

not jut boundless energy, or bone wearying fatigue.

Delve deeper.

You are divinity; the vast and open sky of spirit.

It's the light of God, the ember at your core, the passion and the presence,

the timeless, deathless essence of you that reaches out and touches me.

Who you are transcends fear and turns suffering into liberation.

Who you are is love."

Danna Faulds

ANGEL IN FLIGHT

Jessica

Michael, Michael-John, Valerie,
Celeste, Chanel

Today, Chanel is continuing to grow in independence and we are focusing on developing vocational skills and creating the perfect job for her—a job in which she can utilize her gifts and talents and continue to promote change in our society. (We are doing this with the help of a respite and job coach, who just happens to be one of Chanel's childhood friends. What a blessing it is!)

Respite and Job Coaches

Respite and job coaches are aides that are typically funded through the Regional Center and Department of Rehabilitation to assist adults with disabilities in job training and successfully accessing community-based services. Because this is a paid position, most of these employees are performing their job for the paycheck and are, therefore, not a friend or peer. Sadly, it is typical that, other than family members, special needs individuals only have relationships with paid employees.

But our case was different.

Alisha grew up with Chanel throughout grade school and had been one of the few friends Chanel had in her life. Because Alisha agreed to take the job as Chanel's job coach and respite worker, Chanel has been able to have a support aide who was not only her teacher and mentor, but also a trusted childhood friend. This has been an irreplaceable gift because we know that we can trust Alisha to take care of Chanel and conduct her job with integrity and fidelity.

After Chanel completed the district's adult program when she was twenty-two, she volunteered two years of her time working at our local animal shelter, doing what she loves most—being with animals. She has grown up with a deep love and connection with horses and began riding when she was eight years old.

I humorously call Chanel the "dog whisperer" because she has a profound way of communicating with dogs. There were countless moments growing up when Chanel would see a dog and immediately want to approach the dog but the owner would say, "Oh, be careful, my dog doesn't like strangers." The next thing I knew, the dog would be wagging its tail and licking Chanel's face at the pure amazement of the owner.

Because of all of my experience supporting special needs angels and their families, I knew the only way Chanel could find a job she would be happy performing was to develop a relationship with a local business owner that had a heart of compassion and would be willing to employ a person with a disability.

I came up with the idea for Chanel to be trained to become a professional dog groomer because of her love for animals, and her special connection with dogs. After a bit of research, I found a local dog groomer who offered a credentialed dog-grooming program, and then I worked with the Department of Rehabilitation and the Regional Center to fund this program for Chanel.

Upon completion of the program, Chanel will be hired to work at the same dog groomer business where she will receive her credential.

As fate would have it, the dog groomer is located less than a mile from our home. And Jamie, the owner, just so happened to have graduated high school in Chanel's graduating class and remembers Chanel from high school. She is an amazing advocate for Chanel's independence and has a profound inclusive nature. She does not see Chanel as "disabled" and her focus is always on Chanel's abilities and great potential.

Can They...Where Will They...Work?

Competitive employment for adults with disabilities is a huge problem for families today. When a student with an IEP no longer requires school district services, most adults end up living with their parents and without services. Parents are at a loss to know what to do to assist their adult child in obtaining a job. Those who know where to turn go to both the Department of Rehabilitation and the Regional Center, government agencies that provide supports and services to special needs adults to find them competitive employment. Yet, in truth, most of the programs that are intended to provide job training and placement will, in fact, never fulfill this promise.

As parents, we are charged with creating our own connections within our community to meet the needs of our kids as adults. We cannot leave this responsibility up to the government agencies, as it simply will not happen. Their typical protocol is to fit each individual into the "box" of services and job placements that are available within their program. This simply does not work. Just as any typical young adult, our adult children are individuals with their own gifts and strengths and specific interests, and the jobs they offered Chanel were completely inappropriate for her as an individual. Because I was knowledgeable about the adult system after experiencing the same challenges with Jessica, once again, I was faced with the reality of a broken system. But this time, I was armed with the skills of a professional advocate and took the steps needed to make the connections and develop the relationships within my community to create an appropriate job placement for Chanel.

Flying with Others...Finally!

"Mommy, guess what? Jamie is going to take me with her employees to Knott's Scary Farm for Halloween!"

We were elated with joy at this inclusive invitation. No one, other than Alisha, Chanel's childhood friend and current job coach, had ever invited Chanel to be included as an adult either. While friends and family's adult children took trips to the mall, went to the movies and out to dinner, Chanel was not remembered.

I was a bit apprehensive to allow Chanel to attend without the assistance of an adult. Until that time, either Alisha or one of our family members was always there to assist her in order to keep her safe in the event of a seizure. My mind went back to the memory of the Camp nightmare and the image of Chanel seizing and alone on the forest ground. But then, I recalled the day Chanel walked home all by herself and declared, "Mom, I am not a little girl anymore! You need to let me grow up!" Although my fears were strong, my trust in Jamie to keep Chanel safe was stronger. Pushing my apprehension aside, I knew I had to take a leap of faith to allow my angel to gain her independence and learn how to take flight in the world.

Chanel came home at 2:30 in the morning, safe and sound, after spending the entire evening at the amusement park with her adult peers. She talked about it for days later, reminiscing about how much fun she had.

It was my angel's reward after years of segregation. She was filled with happiness because she was finally included with her peers and given the opportunity to be an independent adult.

Life is Good

As I close with these final pages of my book, my third daughter, Celeste, is working on her singing career and works at a popular clothing store in our area. And my youngest, Michael-John, is attending Washington State University working toward his masters degree in criminal justice. I continue to enjoy being a grandmother to Jessica's daughter, Symphony, who is now sixteen and soon will graduate high school.

Today, I still consider myself a Christian who has let go of the judgment and limiting rules of organized religion. With an open heart full of wonder, I embrace all religions that focus the spiritual path on the message of oneness, unity, and unconditional love, which is also the true foundation of the Christian faith.

As the ripple of Chanel's message continues to expand, my advocacy work is moving in the direction of becoming a life coach for parents of exceptional children and returning to my passion for speaking about the kids and educational advocacy, as well as work directly with the kids by teaching a special needs Yoga class to help them in balancing their high vibrational energy.

Life is good. Still challenging at times. But good.

I'll be forever grateful to both my angels, Chanel and Jessica, for leading me on this journey, and to my own soul for giving me the courage to find my own wings.

ABOUT VALERIE

Valerie Aprahamian, Founder of Advocates For Angels, is a Non-Attorney Advocate, Author, Special Education Law Teacher, and Speaker who helps parents of special needs children in the development of their children's Individual Education Program (IEP)—to enable each child to reach the highest expression of themselves and fulfill their purpose for being on the planet. As a mother of two special needs children, Valerie has been called to work with families, not only in education but also in awakening to the gifts these special angels can bring into their lives. Her first daughter, Jessica, was diagnosed with ADHD at five years old. At seventeen years old, Jessica became a client of the Regional Center under the eligibility of Epilepsy and received adult services through the Department of Rehabilitation and the Regional Center until she passed away at the age of twenty-eight. Her second daughter, Chanel, was diagnosed with Autism and Seizure Disorder at the age of three. Chanel received Early Intervention services through the Early Start Program and then Special Education services through an IEP until the age of twenty-two. Chanel was the first student with autism to be fully included in a general education classroom in her Local School District, and she graduated with a high school diploma with honors. Chanel continues to receive services through the Regional Center and the Department of Rehabilitation.

In Valerie's experience as a non-attorney advocate for more than eighteen years, she has represented hundreds of families with special needs children, attending close to two thousand IEP meetings. She holds a credential from William and Mary University Special Education Law Institute and attended Grace College of Theology, majoring in Clinical Psychology, and Mount San Antonio College with a focus on Fine Arts. She held a position on the board of the Corona/Norco Unified School District Community Advisory Committee (CAC), MOPS International, Riverside Community College — Child Development

Department, Women's Ministries Canyon Hills Friends Church, and Soroptimist Corona. Her professional development has included credentialed programs and conferences, which include Cure Autism Now (CAN), Speech and Language Development Center, Los Angeles and Inland Empire Autism Society, Team of Advocates for Special Kids (TASK), The Association for Severely Handicapped (TASH), Protection and Advocacy, Area Board 12, Inland Empire and Orange County Regional Center, Corona/Norco Unified Community Advisory Committee (CAC), Future Horizons, Toni Atwood and Carol Gray, Integrated Resources Institute Integration Institute, California Board of Education Sacramento Reauthorization of IDEA.

Valerie worked extensively in creating a disabilities ministry at several churches in her area and founded a FETA group (From Emotions To Advocacy), where she taught special education law for more than ten years. Valerie successfully led a system reform in her local school district to improve the relationships between parents and special education administrators to ensure the provision of FAPE to children on IEP's. Valerie has spoken extensively to teach special education law at Biola University, Canyon Hills Friends Church, Crossroads Christian Center, Olive Branch Community Church, MOPS International, CSP-CCFSP (Community Service Programs-Collaborative Courts Full Service Partnerships), Community College Paraprofessional Project — Riverside Community College, Inland Regional Center, Inland Empire Autism

Society, Corona/Norco Unified School District — Parents Helping Parents.

She resides in Southern California with her husband Michael and her three children, Chanel, Celeste, and Michael-John, and two dogs, Jonas and Bijon. She is a delighted grandmother of Symphony, daughter of Jessica, Valerie's eldest. Valerie is a credentialed Yoga Alliance teacher, as yoga practice is a major component in her spiritual development. She enjoys painting and drawing, gardening and reading, and is an avid beach lover.

A SPECIAL
INVITATION
from Valerie

You've read my story and witnessed what's possible when parents dig in, educate themselves, and take intentional action on behalf of their special needs angel.

And now I want to help you do the same.

To help you get started, I've put together a FREE RESOURCE for you, which includes a Checklist and Important Tips to support you in making your next IEP meeting a powerful, effective experience for you, your special education team, and especially your special needs angel. I call it "How to Get What You Want for Your Special Needs Child."

In order to receive the "How to Get What You Want for Your Special Needs Child" Checklist and Tips, please go to www.AdvocatesForAngels.com and sign up to receive it and all of the important updated resources and support information I'll be sending out on a monthly basis.

On the website, you'll also find a simple way to schedule a consultation with me if you need individualized support through this process.

Book Valerie to Speak

I love to share my story and expertise, and one of my favorite things to do is help parents dig in, get educated, and take intentional action on behalf of their children from stages around the globe.

If you're interested in having me speak to your organization, parent group, or school district, please go to my website (www.AdvocatesForAngels.com) and follow the steps on the "Book Valerie to Speak" page.

Made in the USA
San Bernardino, CA
30 August 2016